AF225997

Climbing a Few of Japan's 100 Famous Mountains –

Volume 1:
Mt. Daisetsu (Mt. Asahidake)

Daniel H. Wieczorek and Kazuya Numazawa

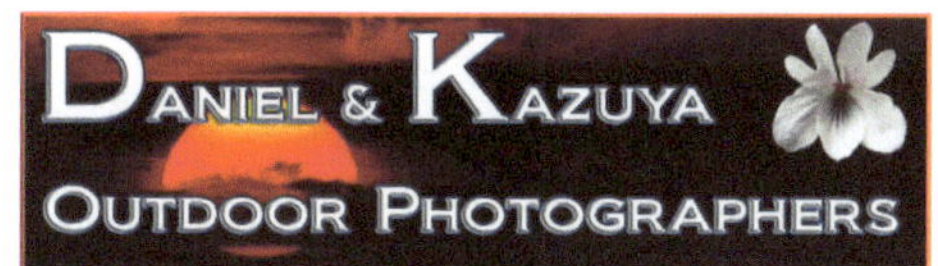

Climbing a Few of Japan's 100 Famous Mountains –

Volume 1:
Mt. Daisetsu (Mt. Asahidake)

ISBN-10: 0996216138
ISBN-13: 978-0-9962161-3-5

Rev. 1

DEDICATION

This work is dedicated, first of all, to my partner, Kazuya Numazawa. He always keeps my interest in photography up and makes me keep striving for the perfect photo. He also often makes me think of the expression "when the going gets tough, the tough keep going." Without my partner it has to also be noted that I most likely would not have climbed any of these mountains.

Secondly, it is dedicated to my mother and father, bless them, for tolerating and even encouraging my photography hobby from the time I was twelve years old.

And, finally, it is dedicated to my friends who have encouraged me to create books of photographs which I have taken while doing mountain climbing.

Other Books in this Series

"Climbing a Few of Japan's 100 Famous Mountains – Volume 2: Mt. Chokai (Choukai)"; ISBN-13: 9781494368401; 72 Pages; Dec. 8, 2013

"Climbing a Few of Japan's 100 Famous Mountains – Volume 3: Mt. Gassan"; ISBN-13: 9781494872175; 70 Pages; January 4, 2014

"Climbing a Few of Japan's 100 Famous Mountains – Volume 4: Mt. Hakkoda & Mt. Zao"; ISBN-13: 9781495396564; 88 Pages; Jan. 31, 2014

"Climbing a Few of Japan's 100 Famous Mountains – Volume 5: Mt. Kumotori"; ISBN-13: 9781495980527; 84 Pages; February 17, 2014

"A Pocket-Size Version of Climbing a Few of Japan's 100 Famous Mountains – Volume 5: Mt. Kumotori"; ISBN-13: 9781497444942; 90 Pages; March 25, 2014

"Climbing a Few of Japan's 100 Famous Mountains – Volume 6: Mt. Shirane (Kusatsu)"; ISBN-13: 9781497303232; 80 Pages; March 11, 2014

"Climbing a Few of Japan's 100 Famous Mountains – Volume 7: Mt. Shibutsu"; ISBN-13: 9781497539273; 80 Pages; April 4, 2014

"Climbing a Few of Japan's 100 Famous Mountains – Volume 8: Mt. Kiso-Komagatake"; ISBN-13: 9781499178630; 72 Pages; April 18, 2014

"Climbing a Few of Japan's 100 Famous Mountains – Volume 9: Mt. Kitadake"; ISBN-13: 9781499786088; 62 Pages; June 4, 2014

"Climbing a Few of Japan's 100 Famous Mountains – Volume 10: Mt. Mizugaki"; ISBN-13: 9781500235284; 70 Pages; June 18, 2014

"Climbing a Few of Japan's 100 Famous Mountains – Volume 11: Mt. Shiroumadake (includes Mt. Shakushidake & Mt. Yarigatake)"; ISBN-13: 9781500463885; 178 Pages; July 9, 2014

"Climbing a Few of Japan's 100 Famous Mountains – Volume 12: Mt. Tate (Tateyama)"; ISBN-13: 9781500946326; 176 Pages; Aug. 26, 2014

"Climbing a Few of Japan's 100 Famous Mountains – Volume 13: Mt. Yatsugatake (Mt. Akadake)"; ISBN-13: 9781502877581; 208 Pages; October 22, 2014

FOREWORD

What is the purpose of this series of books? It is to show you, in photographs, some of the astounding sights and scenery we have seen while climbing the mountains included herein. At this time we have climbed 14 of Japan's 100 Famous Mountains. The ones we have climbed are: 1) Mt. Daisetsu (2,290 m) (大雪山) = Mt. Asahidake (旭岳); 2) Mt. Chokai (2,236 m) (鳥海山); 3) Mt. Gassan (1,984 m) (月山); 4) Mt. Hakkoda (1,584 m) (八甲田山); 5) Mt. Zao (1,841 m) (蔵王山); 6) Mt. Kumotori (2,017 m) (雲取山); 7) Mt. Kusatsu-Shirane (2,171 m) (草津白根山); 8) Mt. Shibutsu (2,228 m) (至仏山); 9) Mt. Kiso-Komagatake (2,956 m) (木曾駒ヶ岳); 10) Mt. Kitadake (North Peak) (3,192 m) (北岳); 11) Mt. Mizugaki (2,230 m) (瑞牆山); 12) Mt. Shiroumadake (2,932 m) (白馬岳); 13) Mt. Tateyama (3,015 m) (立山); and 14) Mt. Yatsugatake (2,899 m) (八ヶ岳).

By the way, I (Daniel) did all of the writing and Kazuya did a fair percentage of the photography. So, do not be surprised from time to time when you see references such as "Kazuya" and "that's me…".

Daniel and Kazuya's ***"Outdoor Photography of Japan: Through the Seasons"*** includes some of the same photos as this work, but this work may be thought of as a subset of that work because that work includes adventures to many mountains beyond the 14 famous mountains which are found in this series of books. In addition, the photos in that book were more than 50% flower photos. This series includes less than 1% flower photos, and only where the flower is a part of a mountain scene. In addition, the majority of the photos you'll find in this series were not included in that work.

TABLE OF CONTENTS

Regions & Prefectures of Japan

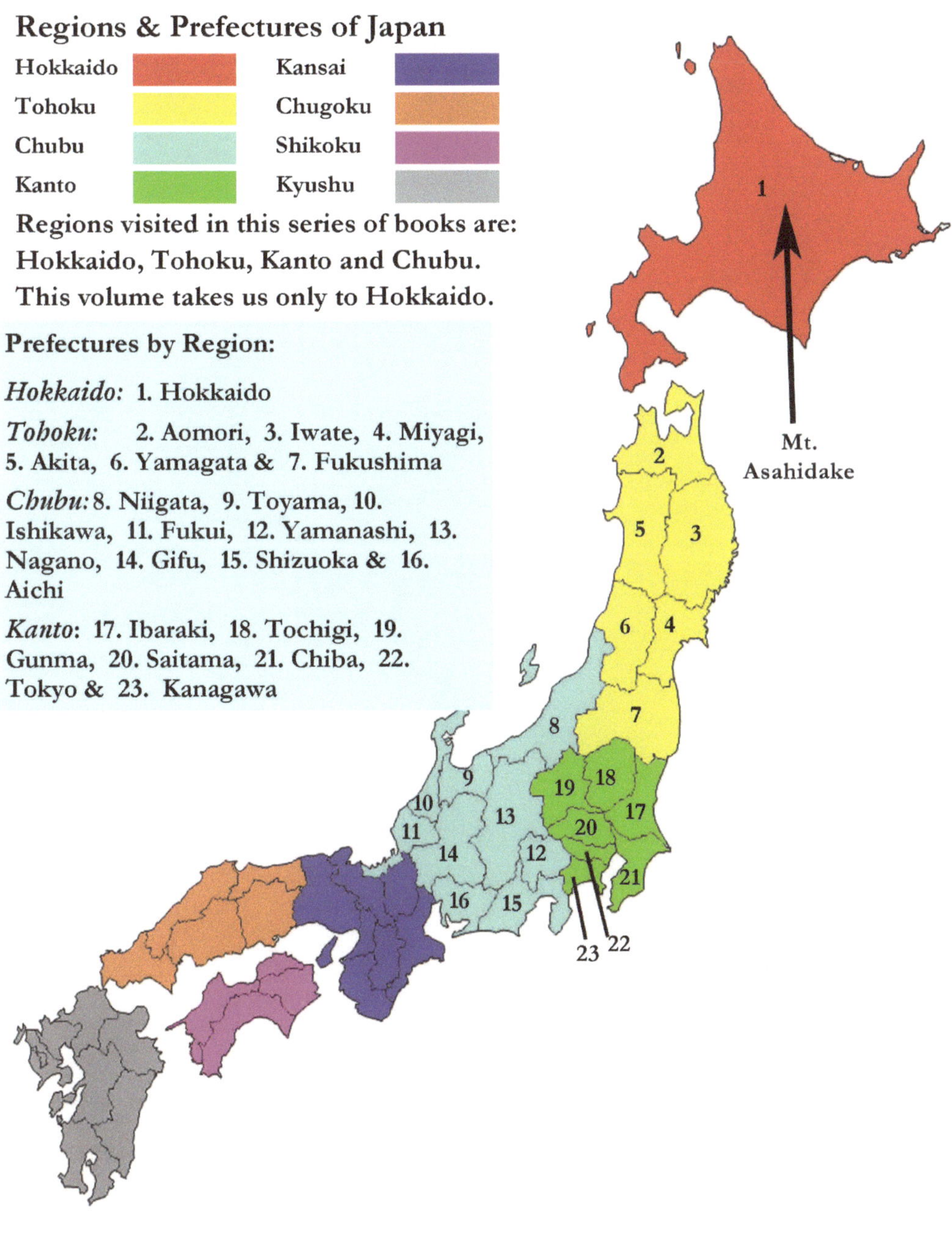

Regions visited in this series of books are:
Hokkaido, Tohoku, Kanto and Chubu.
This volume takes us only to Hokkaido.

Prefectures by Region:

Hokkaido: 1. Hokkaido

Tohoku: 2. Aomori, 3. Iwate, 4. Miyagi, 5. Akita, 6. Yamagata & 7. Fukushima

Chubu: 8. Niigata, 9. Toyama, 10. Ishikawa, 11. Fukui, 12. Yamanashi, 13. Nagano, 14. Gifu, 15. Shizuoka & 16. Aichi

Kanto: 17. Ibaraki, 18. Tochigi, 19. Gunma, 20. Saitama, 21. Chiba, 22. Tokyo & 23. Kanagawa

1) JAPAN'S 100 FAMOUS MOUNTAINS

What are Japan's 100 famous mountains? A selection of famous mountains in Japan has been compiled since the Edo period (1603 – 1867) and the list has been revised several times since the very first list appeared. At the current time the list of 100 famous mountains includes those shown below. Also shown is the Japanese pronunciation, elevation in meters and feet, the Japanese kanji, the Region the mountain is in and a few a.k.a. (also known as) names.

Hokkaido:

1. Mt. Akan (Akandake) 1,499 4,918 阿寒岳
2. **Mt. Asahi (Asahidake) a.k.a.**
    Mt. Daisetsu (Daisetsuzan) **2,290** **7,513** **旭岳**
    a.k.a. (大雪山)
3. Mt. Poroshiri (Poroshiridake) 2,052 6,734 幌尻岳
4. Mt. Rausu (Rausudake) 1,660 5,446 羅臼岳
5. Mt. Rishiri (Rishiridake) 1,721 5,646 利尻岳
6. Mt. Shari (Sharidake) 1,545 5,069 斜里岳
7. Mt. Tokachi (Tochidake) 2,077 6,814 十勝岳
8. Mt. Tomuraushi (Tomuraushiyama) 2,141 7,024
    トムラウシ山
9. Mt. Yotei (Yoteizan) a.k.a.
    (Mt. Shiribeshi) (Shiribeshiyama) 1,893 6,211 羊蹄山
    a.k.a. (後方羊蹄山)

Tohoku Region:

10. Mt. Adatara (Adatarayama) 1,700 5,577
     安達太良山
11. Mt. Aizu-Komagatake (Aizukomagatake)
     2,132 6,995 会津駒ケ岳
12. Mt. Asahi (Asahirenpou) 1,870 6,135 朝日連峰
13. Mt. Azuma (Azumayama) 2,035 6,676 吾妻山
14. Mt. Bandai (Bandaisan) 1,819 5,968 磐梯山
15. **Mt. Chōkai (Chōkaisan)** **2,236** **7,336** **鳥海山**
16. **Mt. Gassan (Gassan)** **1,984** **6,509** **月山**
17. Mt. Hachimantai (Hachimantai) 1,614 5,295 八幡平
18. **Mt. Hakkōda (Hakkōdasan)** **1,584** **5,197** **八甲田山**

19.	Mt. Hayachine (Hayachinesan)	1,917	6,289	早池峰山
20.	Mt. Hiuchigatake (Hiuchigatake)	2,356	7,730	燧ケ岳
21.	Mt. Iide (Iiderenpou)	2,105	6,906	飯豊連峰
22.	Mt. Iwaki (Iwakisan)	1,625	5,331	岩木山
23.	Mt. Iwate (Iwatesan)	2,038	6,686	岩手山
24.	**Mt. Zaō (Zaōsan)**	**1,841**	**6,040**	**蔵王山**

Kanto Region:

25.	Mt. Akagi (Akagiyama)	1,828	5,997	赤城山
26.	Mt. Asama (Asamayama)	2,568	8,425	浅間山
27.	Mt. Azumaya (Azumayasan)	2,354	7,723	四阿山
28.	Mt. Hiragatake (Hiragatake)	2,141	7,024	平ヶ岳
29.	Mt. Hotaka (Hotakayama)	2,158	7,080	武尊山
30.	**Mt. Kumotori (Kumotoriyama)**	**2,017**	**6,617**	**雲取山**
31.	**Mt. Kusatsu-Shirane (Kusatsu-Shiranesan)**			
		2,171	**7,123**	**草津白根山**
32.	Mt. Nantai (Nantaisan)	2,486	8,156	男体山
33.	Mt. Nasu (Nasudake)	1,915	6,283	那須岳
34.	Mt. Nikko-Shirane (Nikko-Shiranesan)	2,578	8,458	日光白根山
35.	Mt. Ryokami (Ryoukamisan)	1,723	5,653	両神山
36.	**Mt. Shibutsu (Shibutsusan)**	**2,228**	**7,310**	**至仏山**
37.	Mt. Sukai (Sukaisan)	2,144	7,034	皇海山
38.	Mt. Tanigawa (Tanigawadake)	1,963	6,440	谷川岳
39.	Mt. Tanzawa (Tanzawasan)	1,567	5,141	丹沢山
40.	Mt. Tsukuba (Tsukubasan)	877	2,877	筑波山

Chubu Region:

41.	Mt. Ainodake (Ainodake)	3,189	10,463	間ノ岳
42.	Mt. Akaishi (Akaishidake)	3,120	10,236	赤石岳
43.	Mt. Amagi (Amagisan)	1,406	4,613	天城山
44.	Mt. Amakazari (Amakazariyama)	1,963	6,440	雨飾山
45.	Mt. Daibosatsu (Daibosatsurei)	2,057	6,749	大菩薩嶺
46.	Mt. Ena (Enasan)	2,191	7,188	恵那山
47.	Mt. Fuji (Fujisan)	3,776	12,388	富士山
48.	Mt. Goryū (Goryūdake)	2,814	9,232	五竜岳
49.	Mt. Hakusan (Hakusan)	2,702	8,865	白山
50.	Mt. Hijiri (Hijiridake)	3,013	9,885	聖岳
51.	Mt. Hiuchi (Hiuchiyama)	2,462	8,077	火打山
52.	Mt. Hōō (Hōōsan)	2,840	9,318	鳳凰山

53.	Mt. Hotaka (Hotakadake)	3,190	10,466	穂高岳
54.	Mt. Jōnen (Jōnendake)	2,857	9,373	常念岳
55.	Mt. Kai-Komagatake (Kaikomagatake)	2,967	9,734	甲斐駒ケ岳
56.	Mt. Kasa (Kasagatake)	2,897	9,505	笠ヶ岳
57.	Mt. Kashima Yarigatake (Kashimayarigatake)			
		2,889	9,478	鹿島槍ヶ岳
58.	Mt. Kinpu (Kinpusan)	2,599	8,527	金峰山
59.	Mt. Kirigamine (Kirigamine)	1,925	6,316	霧ヶ峰
60.	**Mt. Kiso-Komagatake (Kisokomagatake)**			
		2,956	**9,698**	**木曽駒ケ岳**
61.	**Mt. Kitadake (Kitadake)**	**3,192**	**10,472**	**北岳**
62.	Mt. Kobushi (Kobushidake)	2,475	8,120	甲武信岳
63.	Mt. Kuro (Kurodake) a.k.a.			
	(Mt. Suisho) (Suishodake)	2,978	9,770	黒岳
	a.k.a. (水晶岳)			
64.	Mt. Kurobe-Gorō (Kurobegorōdake)	2,840	9,318	黒部五郎岳
65.	Mt. Makihata (Makihatayama)	1,967	6,453	巻機山
66.	**Mt. Mizugaki (Mizugakiyama)**	**2,230**	**7,316**	**瑞牆山**
67.	Mt. Myoko (Myokosan)	2,454	8,051	妙高山
68.	Mt. Naeba (Naebasan)	2,145	7,037	苗場山
69.	Mt. Norikura (Norikuradake)	3,026	9,928	乗鞍岳
70.	Mt. Ontake (Ontakesan)	3,067	10,062	御嶽山
71.	Mt. Senjōgatake (Senjōgatake)	3,033	9,951	仙丈ケ岳
72.	Mt. Shiomi (Shiomidake)	3,047	9,997	塩見岳
73.	**Mt. Shiroumadake (Shiroumadake)**	**2,932**	**9,619**	**白馬岳**
74.	Mt. Takatsuma (Takatsumayama)	2,353	7,720	高妻山
75.	Mt. Tateshina (Tateshinayama)	2,530	8,301	蓼科山
76.	**Mt. Tateyama (Tateyama)**	**3,015**	**9,892**	**立山**
77.	Mt. Tekari (Tekaridake)	2,591	8,501	光岳
78.	Mt. Tsurugi (Tsurugidake)	2,999	9,839	剱岳
79.	Mt. Uonuma-Komagatake a.k.a.			
	(Echigo-Komagatake)	2,003	6,572	魚沼駒ヶ岳
	a.k.a. (越後駒ケ岳)			
80.	Mt. Utsugi (Utsugidake)	2,864	9,396	空木岳
81.	Mt. Warusawa (Warusawadake)	3,141	10,305	悪沢岳
82.	Mt. Washiba (Washibadake)	2,924	9,593	鷲羽岳
83.	Mt. Yake (Yakedake)	2,444	8,018	焼岳

84.	Mt. Yakushi (Yakushidake)	2,926	9,600	薬師岳
85.	Mt. Yarigatake (Yarigatake)	3,180	10,433	槍ヶ岳
86.	**Mt. Yatsugatake (Yatsugatake)**	**2,899**	**9,511**	**八ヶ岳**
87.	Utsukushigahara Highland			
	(Utsukushigahara)	2,034	6,673	美ヶ原

Western Japan:

88.	Mt. Arashima (Arashimadake)	1,523	4,997	荒島岳
89.	Mt. Aso (Asosan)	1,592	5,223	阿蘇山
90.	Mt. Daisen (Daisen)	1,729	5,673	大山
91.	Mt. Ibuki (Ibukiyama)	1,377	4,518	伊吹山
92.	Mt. Ishizuchi (Ishizuchisan)	1,982	6,503	石鎚山
93.	Mt. Kaimon (Kaimondake)	924	3,031	開聞岳
94.	Mt. Kirishima (Kirishimayama)	1,700	5,577	霧島山
95.	Mt. Kujū (Kujūsan)	1,791	5,876	九重山
96.	Mt. Miya-no-ura (Miyanouradake)	1,936	6,352	宮之浦岳
97.	Mt. Ōmine (Ōminesan)	1,915	6,283	大峰山
98.	Mt. Sobo (Sobosan)	1,756	5,761	祖母山
99.	Mt. Tsurugi (Tsurugisan)	1,955	6,414	剣山
100.	The Wide Mountain of Ōdai			
	(Ōdaigaharayama)	1,695	5,561	大台ケ原山

My partner and I have climbed (or in one, case merely ascended) the fourteen mountains which are **shaded, underlined and in bold** text. You'll probably note that we have not climbed Mt. Fuji and wonder why? The reason is simple – too many people and not enough interesting sights.

Using photographs and a minimum amount of text we will tell (show) you the stories of climbing the fourteen mountains shown above. We will start at the beginning of the 100 mountains list and work our way through it. That means that the first climb we will show you, in this volume, is on Hokkaido and it's a climb of Mt. Daisetsu (2,290.9 m = 7,516 ft) (大雪山), which is also known as Mt. Asahidake. Mt. Daisetsu is the name of the entire mountain range, while Mount Asahi (旭岳 Asahidake) is the tallest mountain in that mountain range and also the tallest mountain in Hokkaido Prefecture, Japan. It is part of the Daisetsuzan Volcanic Group and it is located in the northern part of Daisetsuzan National Park.

The second mountain we'll show you is in the Tohoku Region and the mountain name is Mt. Chokai (or Choukai) (2,236 m = 7,336 ft) (鳥海山). Mt. Chokai is located on the southern border of Akita Prefecture and the northern border of Yamagata Prefecture. It is still an active volcano and it is the second tallest mountain in the Tohoku Region of Japan.

The third mountain is also in the Tohoku Region and it is Mt. Gassan (1,984 m = 6,509 ft) (月山). Mt. Gassan is the highest peak in the Dewa Sanzan trio of sacred mountains. It lies between Mt. Chokai to the north, and Mt. Asahi to the south, in Yamagata Prefecture. Being a sacred mountain, it is famous for the shrine at the summit and in the summer you can often see large groups of white-clothed pilgrims hiking to or from the summit.

The fourth mountain we will show you is also in the Tohoku Region of Japan and the mountain will be Mt. Hakkoda (1,584 m = 5,197 ft) (八甲田山). The Hakkoda Mountains are a volcanic mountain range that lie south of Aomori City, in Aomori Prefecture Japan. The peak name is actually Mt. Hakkoda – Odake. Odake is the tallest peak in the Hakkoda Range.

The fifth mountain we'll show you is Mt. Zao (1,841 m = 6,040 ft) (蔵王山). It is also in the Tohoku Region and also in Yamagata Prefecture. We did not actually make it to the summit of this mountain. We visited it in the winter and it was very cold and windy. We took an automobile as far as possible and then transferred to a gondola car and went only a little bit beyond the top of the gondola – to about the 1,661 m (= 5,449 ft) level of the mountain. We do, however, have some impressive photos from that trip.

The sixth mountain you'll see in this series of books will be Mt. Kumotori (2,017.7 m = 6,620 ft) (雲取山). This is in the Kanto Region and the peak divides the prefectures of Tokyo, Yamanashi and Saitama. Its summit is the highest point in Tokyo. It separates the Okutama Mountains and the Okuchichibu Mountains. No matter which direction you choose to come to this mountain from, the summit is a long hike from the nearest bus stop, road end or train station.

The seventh mountain will be Mt. Kusatsu-Shirane (2,171 m = 7,123 ft) (草津白根山). This peak is also in the Kanto Region of Japan, in Gunma Prefecture. It is called Mt. Kusatsu-Shirane to differentiate it from Mt. Nikko-Shirane, which is on the opposite side of Gunma Prefecture. There is a beautifully colored volcanic pond here known as Yugama. Another volcanic pond close-by is Yumiike and there is a dry crater named Karagama Crater.

The eighth mountain, also in the Kanto Region, in Gunma Prefecture, will be Mt. Shibutsu (2,228 m = 7,310 ft) (至仏山). It separates Oze Marsh (Oze National Park) from the remainder of Gunma Prefecture. It is an interesting mountain composed primarily of serpentinite. There is also a lesser peak known as Mt. Koshibutsu (2,162 m = 7,093 ft).

The ninth mountain we'll take you to is Mt. Kiso-Komagatake (2,956 m = 9,698 ft) (木曾駒ヶ岳). It can be found in Nagano Prefecture, in the Chubu Region. It is located in Japan's Central Alps Mountain Range and is the highest peak in that range.

Then we'll very briefly take you to the tenth of Japan's 100 famous mountains which we have climbed – Mt. Kitadake (North Peak) (3,193 m = 10,476 ft) (北岳). This is Japan's second highest mountain after Mt. Fuji and is known as "the Leader of the Southern Alps". It is in Yamanashi Prefecture, in the Chubu Region.

Mt. Mizugaki (2,230 m = 7,317 ft) (瑞牆山) is the eleventh mountain that will be addressed in this series of books. It too is in the Chubu Region. It is in Yamanashi Prefecture. It lies across the valley from the Southern Alps, slightly southeast of Yatsugatake and northwest of the Daibosatsu ridgeline. Granite towers, blocks and obelisks protrude from the summit of this mountains. It is truly an amazing sight to see from its lower slopes.

Then we'll continue on to the twelfth mountain and that is also in the Chubu Region. It is Mt. Shiroumadake (2,932 m = 9,620 ft) (白馬岳). It is the tallest peak in the Hakuba section of the Hida Mountains, also known as Japan's Northern Alps Mountain Range. It is in Nagano Prefecture.

After that, for the thirteenth mountain, we'll take you to another Chubu Region mountain – Mt. Tateyama (3,015 m = 9,892 ft) (立山). It can be found in the southeastern portion of Toyama Prefecture and it also is a mountain in the Northern Alps Mountain Range, or Hida Mountains. It is one of the tallest peaks in the Hida Mountains and is the highest peak in Toyama Prefecture.

The fourteenth and final mountain we'll cover in this series of books is also in the Chubu Region – Mt. Yatsugatake (Mt. Akadake – 2,899 m = 9,511 ft) (八ヶ岳). Yatsugatake means "eight peaks" and the highest mountain in this range is Mt. Akadake. Actually there are many more than eight peaks, but in Japanese the kanji character for Hachi (八) sometimes implies "many" or "several.

According to legend, Yatsugatake was once higher than Mount Fuji, but Konohana-Sakuyahime, the goddess of Mount Fuji, tore it down out of jealousy, leaving the collection of peaks we have today. This could possibly be true considering that Yatsugatake is older than Fuji and as Fuji rose in prominence Yatsugatake wore away.

Another version of this legend says that a long time ago, Yatsugatake was an ordinary mountain with only one peak, and it was as high as or higher then Mt. Fuji. Yatsugatake's god and Mt. Fuji's goddess began quarreling over their height. Each of them insisted that he/she was taller. The Amitabha Buddha, who was entrusted to arbitrate the dispute, set a valley between the tops of the two mountains and filled it with water. The water submerged the summit of Mt. Fuji, revealing that Yatsugatake was indeed, taller. Mt. Fuji's goddess, who was unyielding, was very angry so she kept striking Yatsugatake with a long stick until it was divided into several peaks, all lower than Mt. Fuji. That is why Mt. Yatsugatake now has so many peaks. Interesting!

By the way – *dake* or *take* (岳) = peak or high peak. Some authors prefer to leave this term off when referring to a Japanese mountain, for example they will refer to Mt. Kitadake as Mt. Kita and use the argument that it is redundant to use the –dake portion of the name. We prefer to use the dake suffix for completeness. If one is to be absolutely correct it should probably be called Kita Peak, not Mt. Kita.

"Mountains are the cathedrals where I practice my religion."
— Anatoli Boukreev

"Climb the mountains and get their good tidings. Nature's peace will flow into you as sunshine flows into trees. The winds will blow their own freshness into you, and the storms their energy, while cares will drop away from you like the leaves of Autumn."
— John Muir, The Mountains of California

"Chasing angels or fleeing demons, go to the mountains."
— Jeffrey Rasley

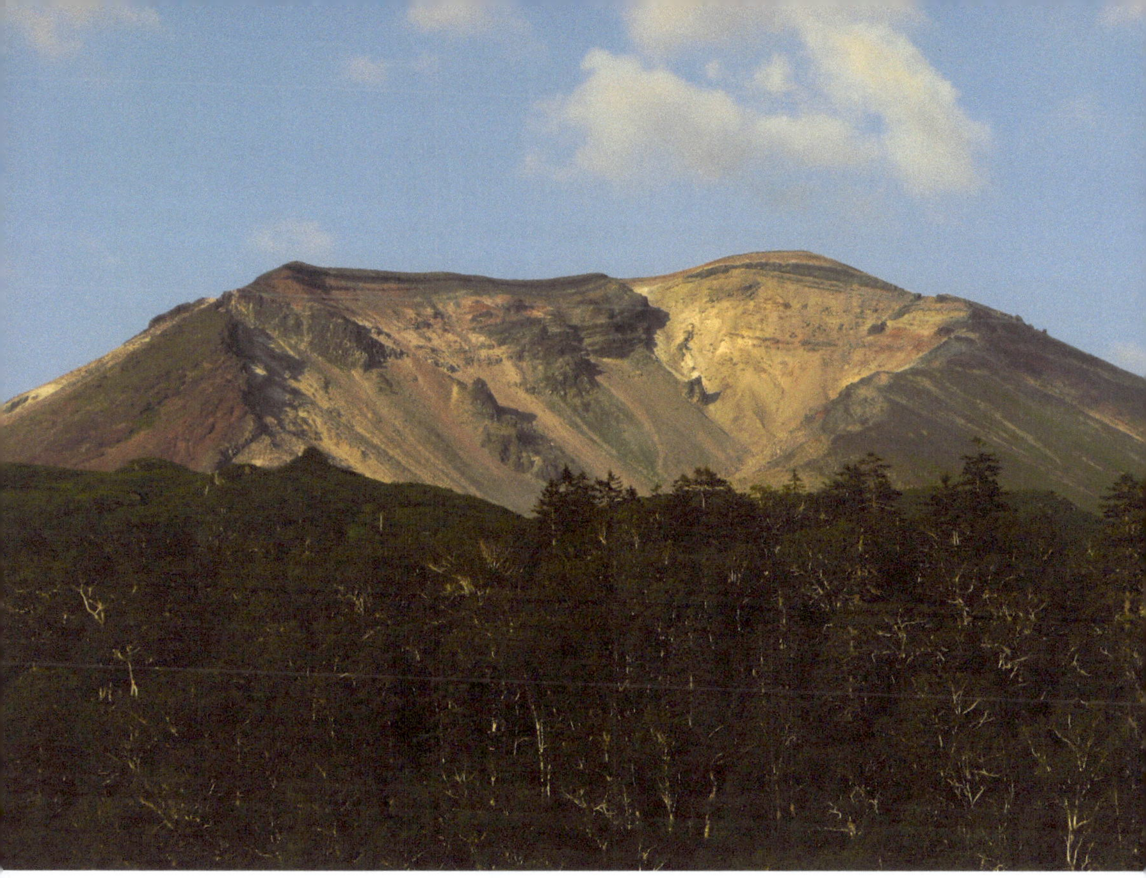

2) MT. DAISETSU (MT. ASAHIDAKE)

The first climb we will show you is on Hokkaido and it's a climb of Mt. Daisetsu (2,290.9 m = 7,516 ft) (大雪山), which is also known as Mt. Asahidake. Mount Asahi or Mt. Asahidake (旭岳) is the tallest mountain in Hokkaido Prefecture, Japan. It is part of the Daisetsuzan Volcanic Group and it is located in the northern part of Daisetsuzan National Park.

We have visited Daisetsuzan National Park two times. The first time was in August 2009 and on that visit we climbed Mt. Asahidake (2,291 m = 7,516 ft) and Mt. Mamiyadake (2,185 m = 7,169 ft) (間宮岳). We arrived at the Youth Hostel, where we would stay, on August 9th, and we climbed the two peaks mentioned just above on August 10th. We left on August 11th. Our stay was short, and we had good weather.

The photo above was taken in 2009 and it shows the summit area of Mt. Asahidake from the bottom of the Mt. Asahidake Ropeway. The weather was exquisite when this photo was taken at 5:44 PM on August 9th. You'll notice that subtle sunset colors are just beginning.

Our second visit was in 2010. We climbed for four days on that trip. The first day, August 7th, we started from the Mt. Kurodake (1,984 m = 6,509 ft) (黒岳) side of Daisetsuzan National Park and summited Mt. Kurodake and then spent the night at the Mt. Kurodake Stone Hut. On the second day we climbed Mt. Hokkaidake (2,149 m = 7,051 ft) (北海岳) and Mt. Hakuundake (2,230 m = 7,315 ft) (白雲岳). On the third day we summited Mt. Hokuchindake (2,244 m = 7,362 ft) (北鎮岳) and Mt. Nakadake (2,113 m = 6,932 ft) (中岳). Then on our fourth day we summited Mt. Asahidake (旭岳) (2,291 m = 7,516 ft), for our second time, Mt. Araidake (2,183 m = 7,162 ft) (荒井岳) and Mamiyadake (2,185 m = 7,169 ft) (間宮岳), for our second time.   On the fifth day we headed back towards home. On this trip we had a fair amount of rainy weather, but we still had an amazing adventure and enjoyed ourselves very much.

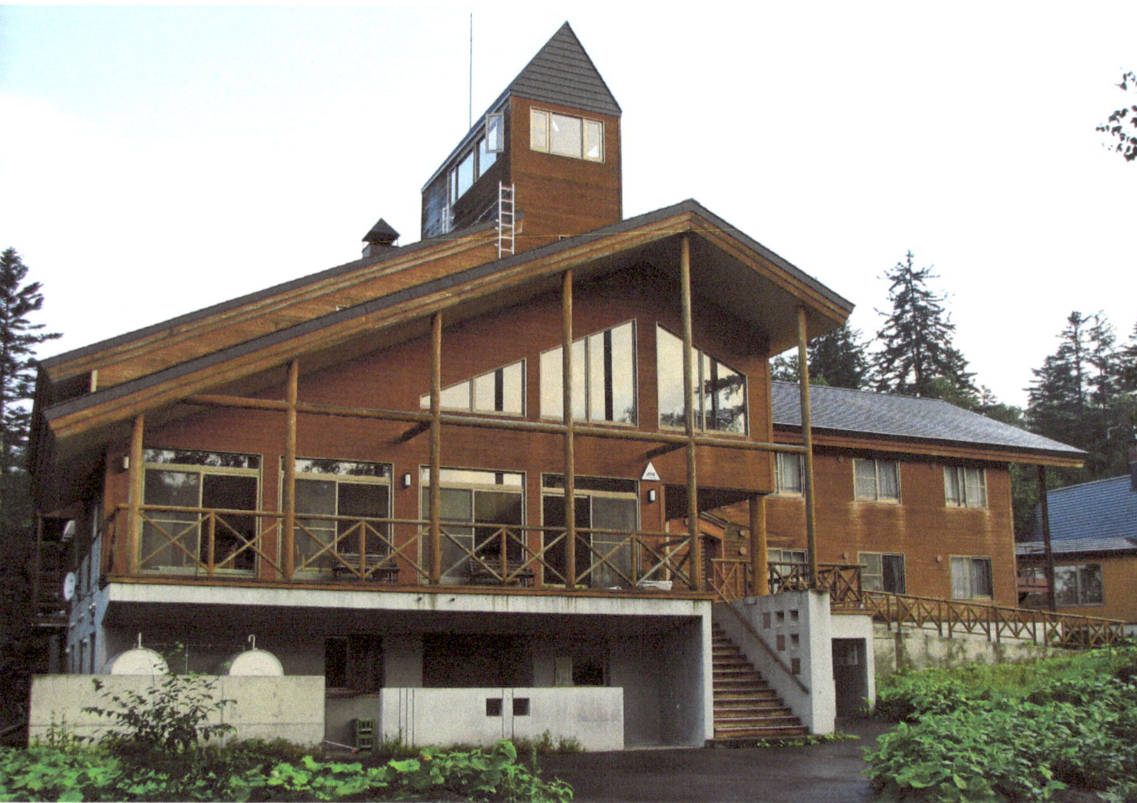

The photo immediately above shows the Youth Hostel where we stayed – the name of it is Daisetsuzan Shirakaba-Sou. It offers very decent meals, a small hot spring, the lookout room at the top, where you can see the summit of Mt. Asahidake, a variety of books and magazines you can peruse while you are staying here and, of course, it offers both dormitory style rooms and also private rooms for families or couples. It is a very nice place to stay.

Now that you have had a brief introduction to Mt. Asahidake we'd like to show you more of the details of the 2010 adventure and therefore we'll now go to the opposite side of Daisetsuzan National Park and start with our ascent of Mt. Kurodake and the adventure from that point.

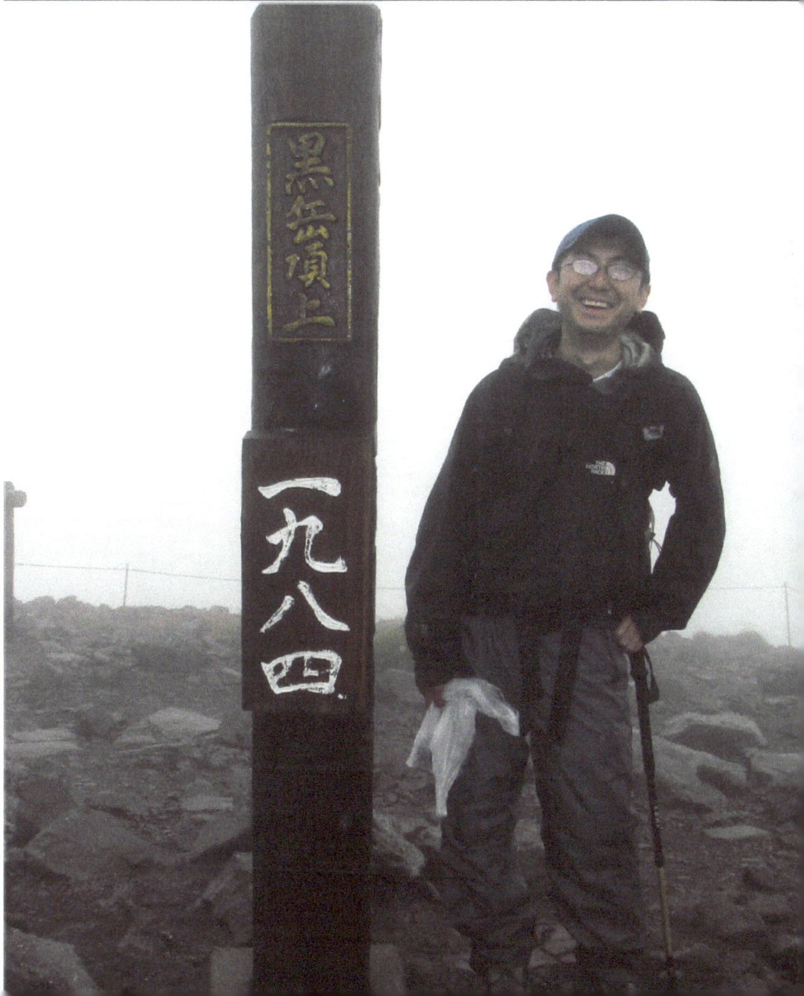

The image to the right shows two separate photographs showing each of us at the summit of Mt. Kurodake (1,984 m = 6,509 ft). As you can see, the weather was not very nice to us as we climbed to the summit of this peak; in fact it was downright miserable, heavy rain, clouds passing by, strong wind and rather cold. But, you should no-

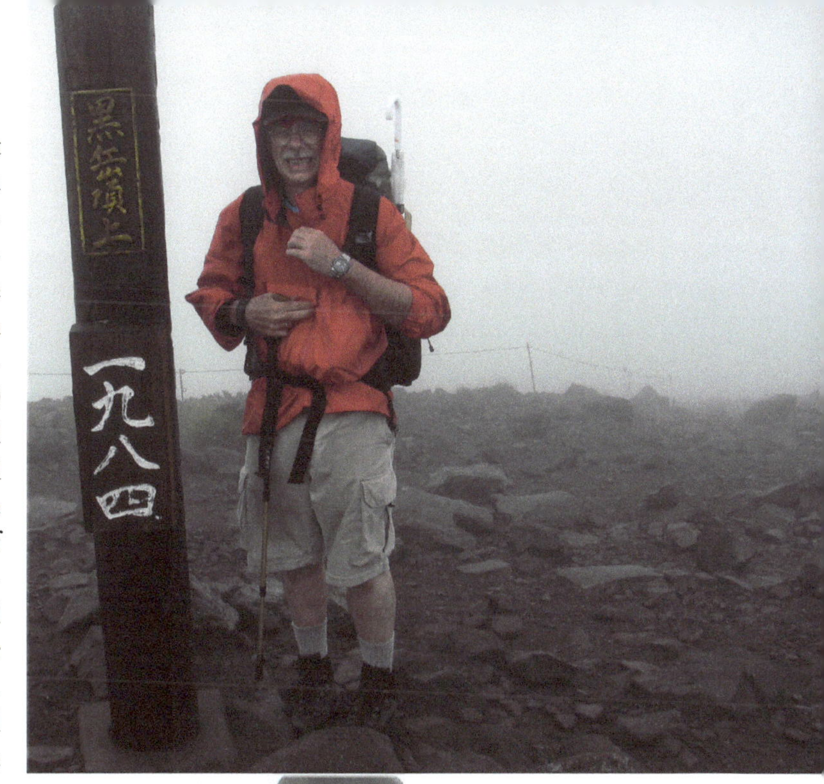

tice that both of us are wearing big smiles despite the terrible weather. We truly enjoy ourselves when we are climbing mountains, and the weather, well – sometimes it slows us down, but not all of the time.

From the summit of Mt. Kurodake we hiked across some interesting country to get to the Kurodake Stone Hut, which is shown in the photo below. You can see why this is called the "Stone Hut" – it's made of rocks! They do not furnish meals at this hut, so we had to bring our own camping stove, fuel and food. They had plenty of water though, and they rented sleeping bags, so we did not have to carry a sleeping bag with us. We stayed at this hut for two nights, as we hiked and climbed from this hut via trails more or less to the south on the first day. Then, on the second day we were going to be hiking trails which would take us more west than south from this point.

As this area is a rather wide and flat plain at around the 1,500 meter level we cannot even begin to imagine how vicious the winters must be at this location. It is completely understandable that the hut has to be built of rock. It is rather surprising that they do not have large rocks on the roof to keep it from blowing away in the storms of winter.

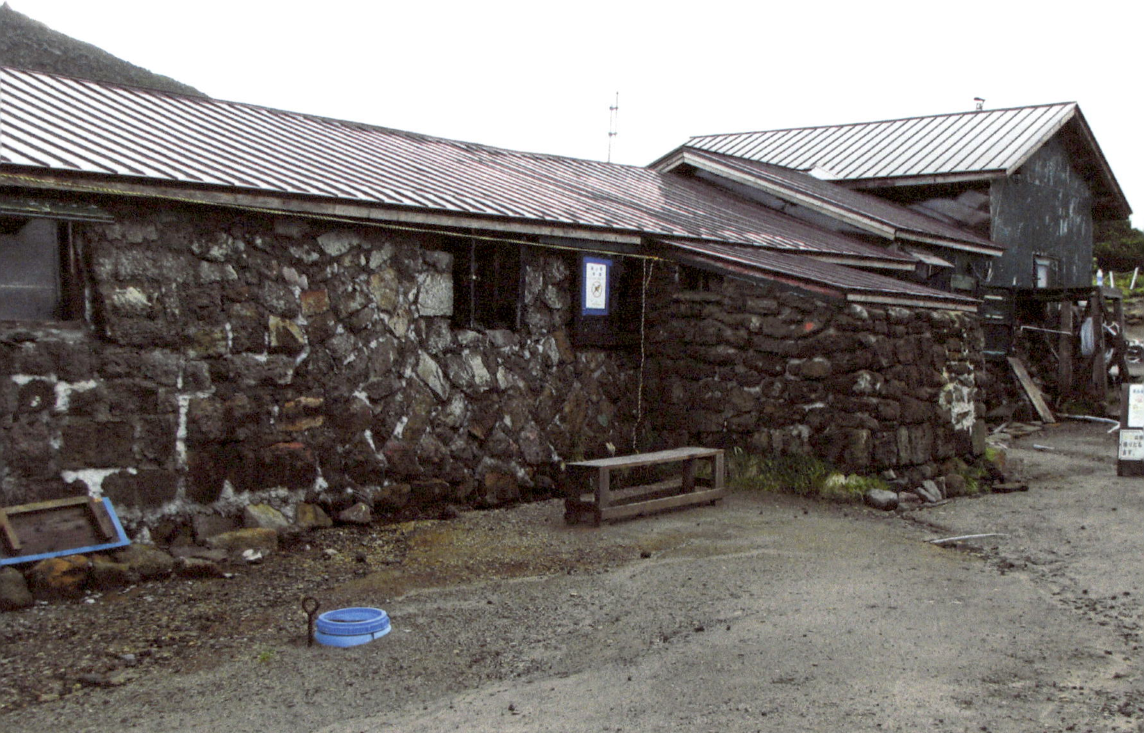

So, tomorrow we'll hike to and climb Mt. Hokkaidake (2,149 m = 7,051 ft) and Mt. Hakuundake (2,230 m = 7,315 ft). The rain will continue, off and on, as will the wind. We'll just do our best though, and have a good time hiking and climbing in the wind and rain; that will be no huge nor insurmountable problem. We traveled a long ways to get here, we cannot let this weather put a damper on either our spirits or on our enjoyment of what we are doing.

On the following page is a small portion of a map which we bought for this adventure. In the upper right hand corner you'll notice the "start here" notation and then you'll see Mr. Kuro (the "dake" suffix has been omitted from all names on this map to keep it a little cleaner). Then you can see the notation for the Mt. Kurodake Hut; that's the photo on the previous page. Off, generally to the south you'll notice Mt. Hokkai(dake) and also Mt. Hakuun(dake). Those are the two peaks we'll hike to and climb tomorrow. Then we will return here for tomorrow night's sleep. On the following day we'll take the trail more to the west and hike to and climb Mt. Hokuchin(dake) and Mt. Naka(dake), continue past Nakadake Hot Spring and take the trail to the "end here" notation. Mt. Hokuchindake is the second highest peak on Hokkaido. Then, for the fourth, and final day, we'll take the ropeway back up and climb Mt. Asahi(dake), Mt. Arai(dake) and Mt. Mamiya(dake). After that we'll again pass Nakadake Hot Spring and end the day at the "end here" notation.

In our four days of hiking and climbing we have no idea how many kilometers or miles we hiked, but it was a lot of them. We also have no idea how many meters we climbed, but again, it was a considerable number.

I can remember once, long ago, reading somewhere that the fifth day of high peak climbing is kind of a magical day in that your heart stops beating as fast, you don't get winded as easily and in general, your body is suddenly in condition for it. Well, I can say that the fourth day is equally as magical – and for the same reasons. On the fourth day we were climbing at a much faster rate than we've ever climbed in our lives, and at the same time, breathing was a lot less difficult than it had ever been before. We felt so good that we never wanted to stop climbing.

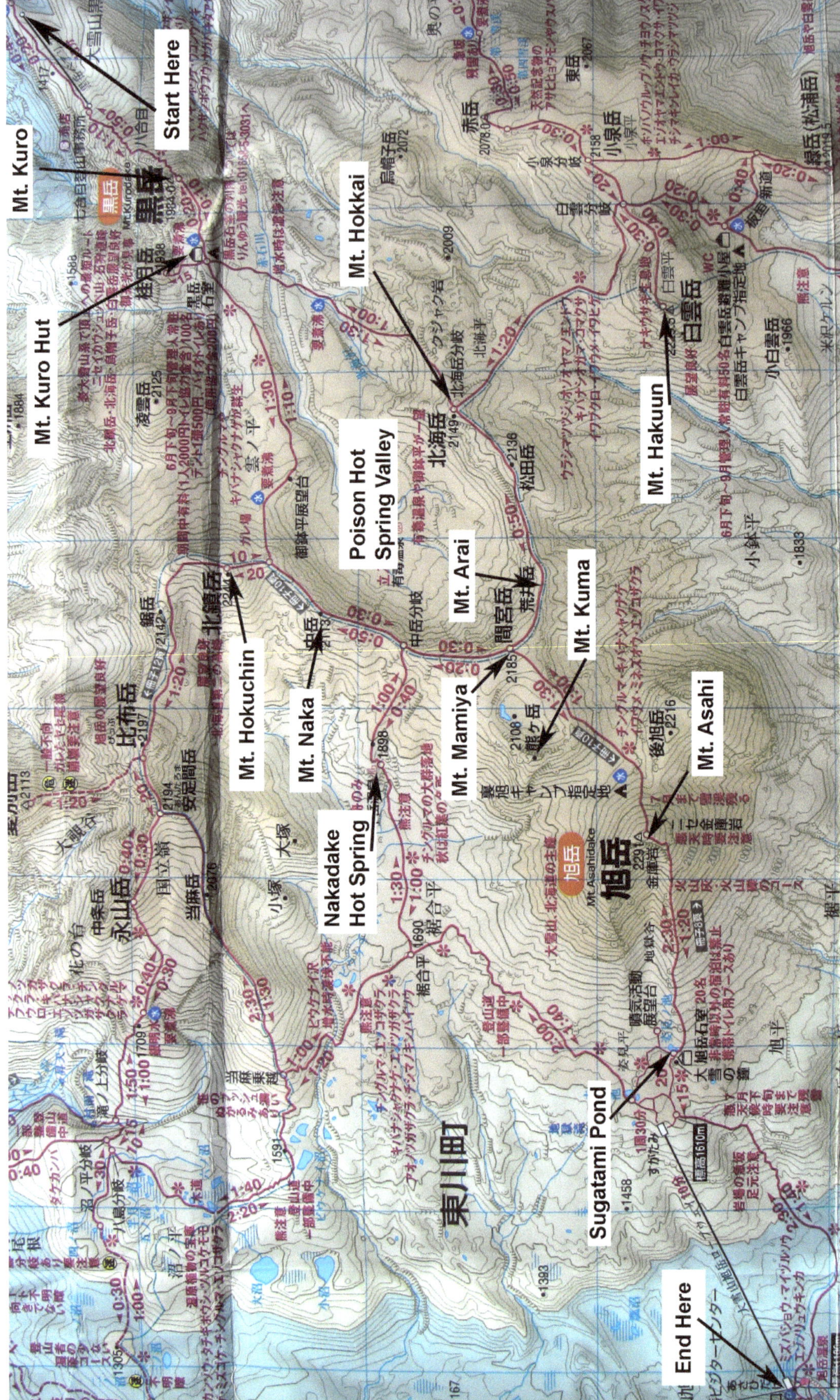

Start Here
Mt. Kuro
Mt. Kuro Hut
Mt. Hokkai
Mt. Hakuun
Poison Hot Spring Valley
Mt. Hokuchin
Mt. Naka
Mt. Arai
Mt. Mamiya
Mt. Kuma
Mt. Asahi
Nakadake Hot Spring
Sugatami Pond
End Here

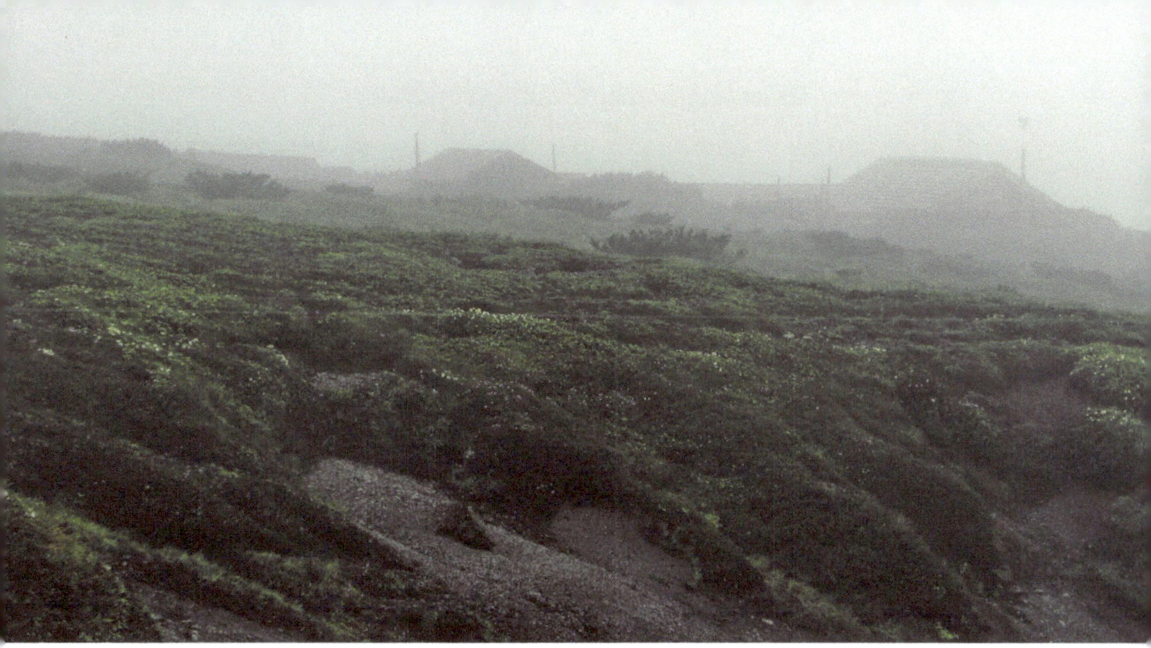

In the photo immediately above you can see what the weather was like when we were leaving the Kurodake Stone Hut on the following morning – you can see the hut in this photo, but not very well. Can you find the two buildings in this photo?

Then, after we hiked just a short distance, however, the sun began to come out and we were given this beautiful green view shown below. It was so amazing to see such green beauty after the previously cloudy skies.

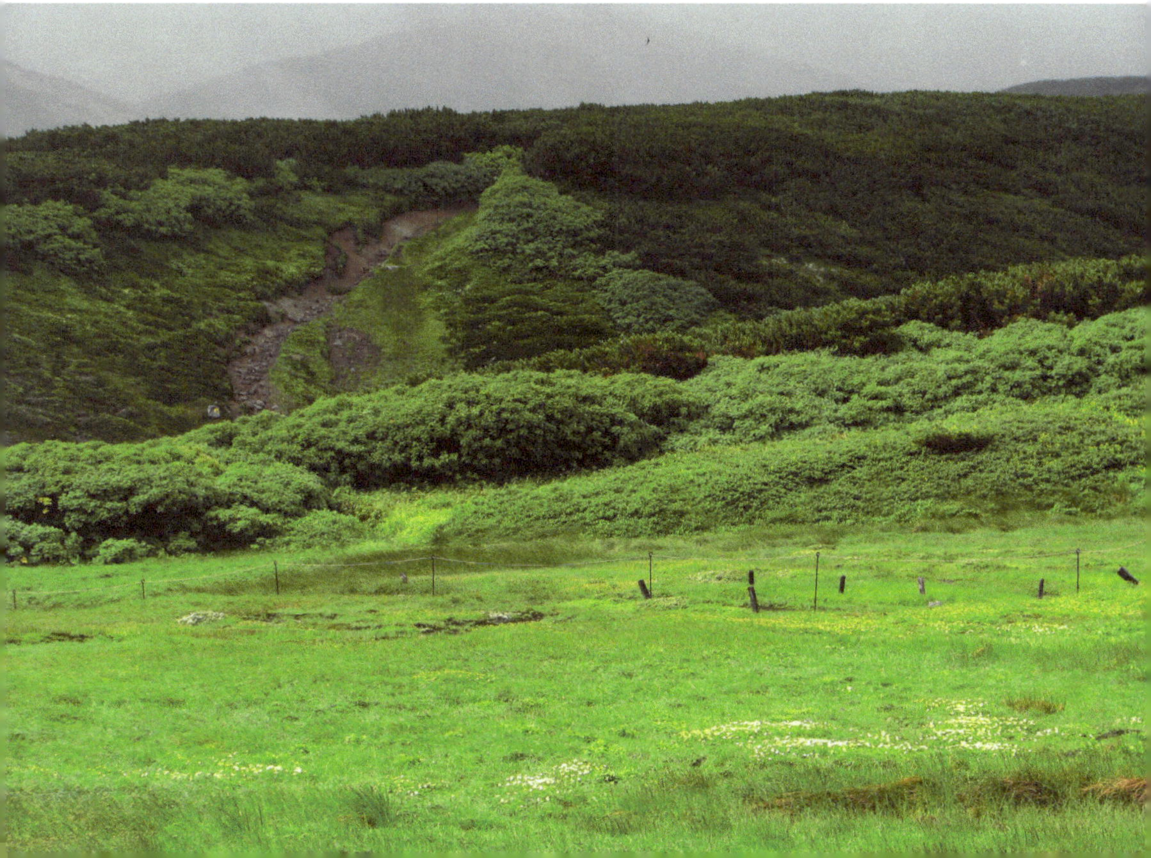

After a few more minutes, or maybe an hour – we weren't watching our clocks nor worried about the time – we came to this large creek, or maybe it's a river. If you go back to the map on Page 14 and find the Mt. Kurodake Hut and then "Poison Hot Spring Valley" and Mt. Hokkaidake you will notice the stream that flows out of "Poison Hot Spring Valley". This is that stream. There was a very strong sulfur smell coming from the water and you can see that the water color is rather milky in appearance. The map gives a strong warning not to go into "Poison Hot Spring Valley" because some of the hot springs there are giving off poisonous gases. We could believe it after smelling this stream. We were a little concerned as to whether the water was acidic enough to present a danger to our boots or to our skin if it soaked through our boots. So, we did our best to keep to the rocks and get as little of this water on us as possible.

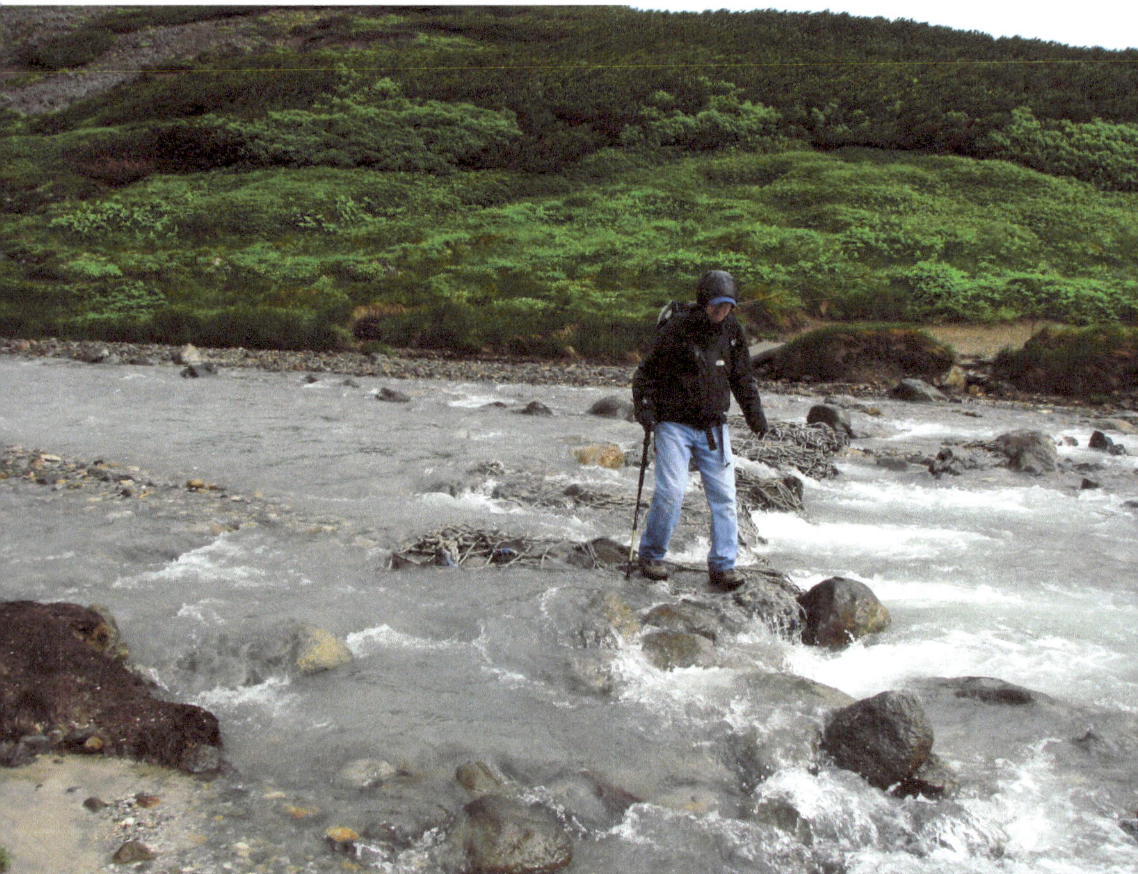

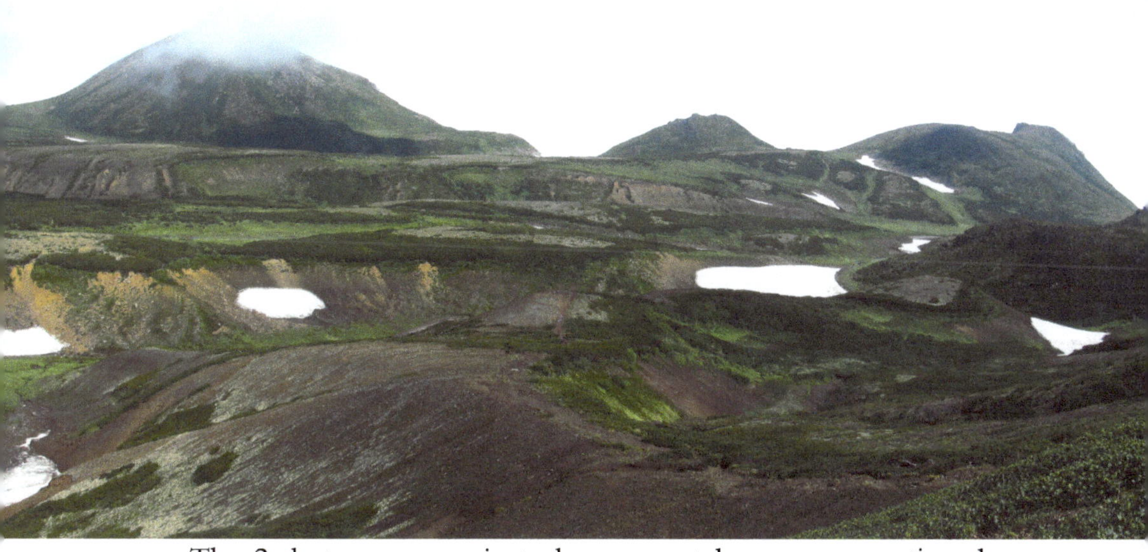

The 2-shot panorama just above was taken as we continued our hike towards Hokkaidake. The mountain closest to the center, with the two small bumps on it, is Mt. Kurodake, the one which we passed over yesterday on our way to the Kurodake Hut. This shot exhibits such beautiful shades of green – it's hard to imagine without actually being there.

The photo immediately below shows a snowfield which we skirted by on our way to the summit of Mt. Hokkaidake. Note the steam rising from it.

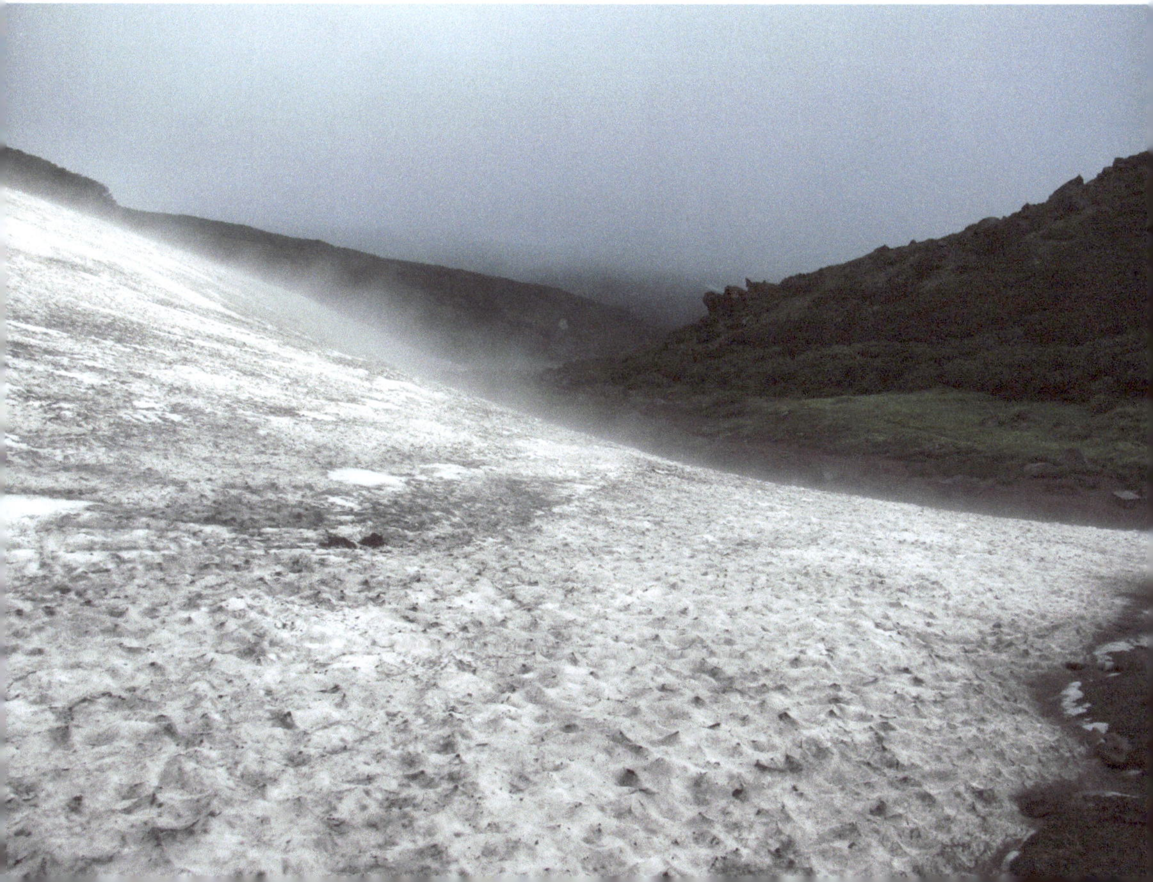

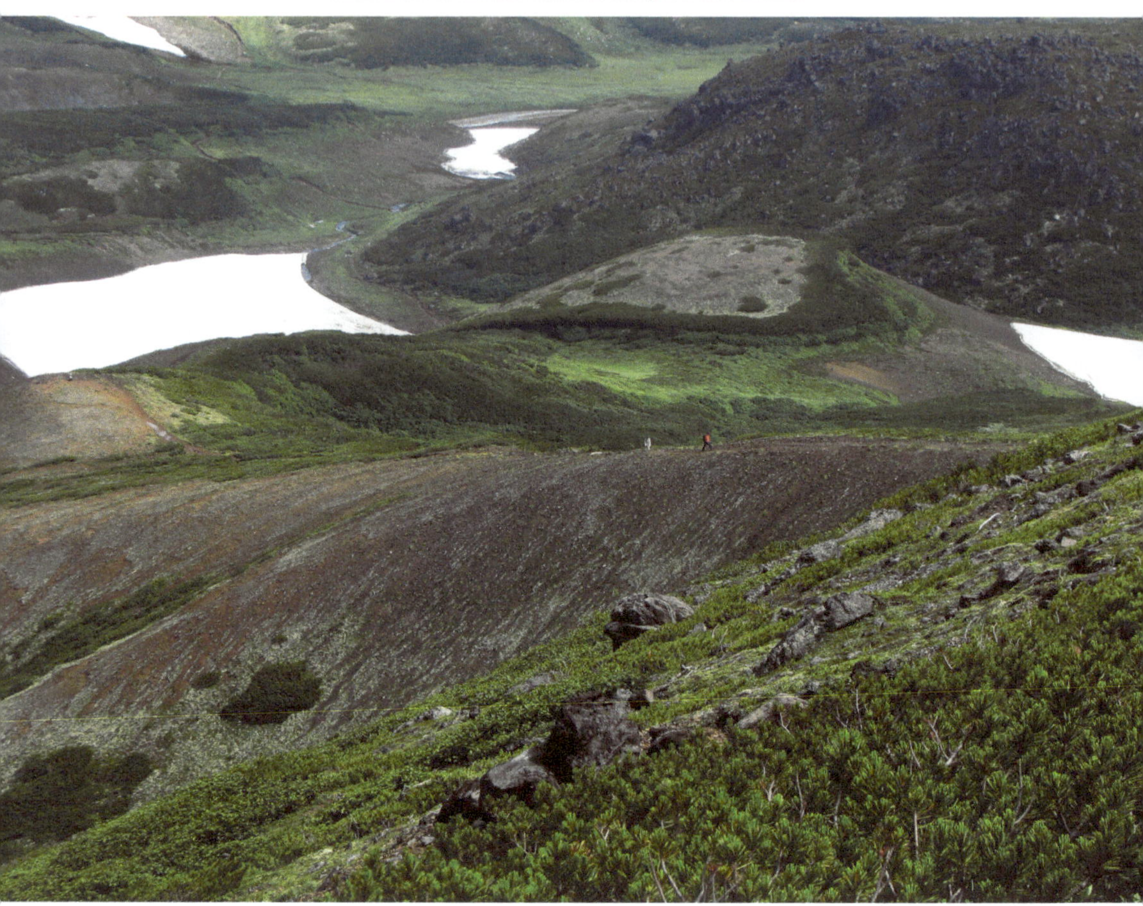

Now (above photo) we are ascending the final major slope before attaining the summit of Mt. Hokkaidake. In this photo you can see two other hikers coming up the trail behind us and if you study this photo closely you can see the trail and the snow field which we skirted by (previous photo). You can see all the way back to the creek flowing out of "Poison Hot Spring Valley," but you cannot see the point at which we crossed that creek. Right this moment the weather is quite nice, but it will probably not stay this way for long. We have to take these photos when we have the opportunity. We have passed a great number of amazing flowers which we have photographed, but this book will not show any photos of flowers. If you want to see the flowers then we encourage you to see our book **"Outdoor Photography of Japan: Through the Seasons"**. This same area is shown in that book — along with the flowers we passed by as we climbed.

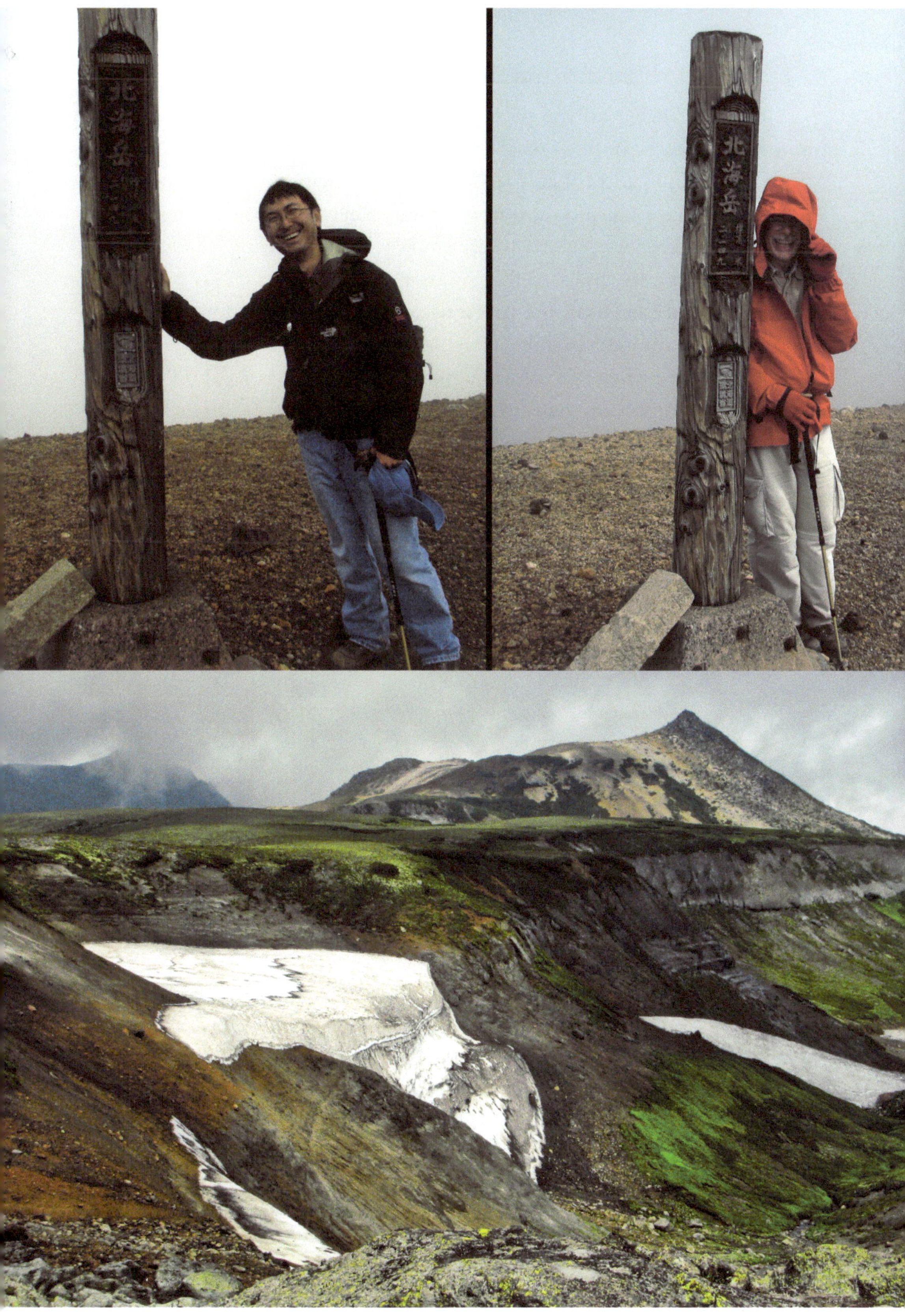

The top image on the previous page is composed of two separate photos which show both of us at the summit of Mt. Hokkaidake (2,149 m = 7,051 ft). You can probably deduce, without being told, that the wind was blowing like a banshee and it was pretty chilly, but you can again see that we both have virtually ear-to-ear smiles. We are feeling good and we are happy to have reached our first summit of the day.

The lower photo on the previous page is a scenery shot which was taken as we continued to hike from Mt. Hokkaidake towards Mt. Hakuundake. The primary reason this photo is included is to show the incredible snow depth in that small valley on the left side of the photo. Keep in mind that this was August. Maybe you can guess that the snow never totally leaves this mountain. You can see that there are many shadows passing over the ground in this photo. The clouds kept blowing around and the conditions were quite cold and very windy. The rain had mostly stopped by this point though.

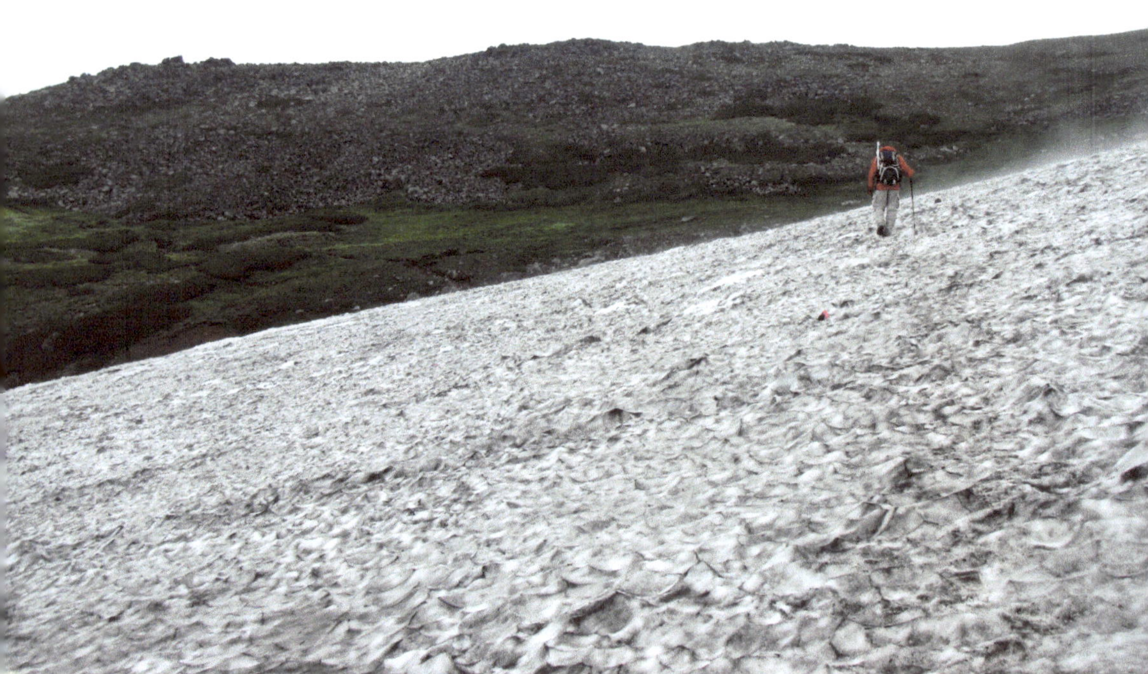

The previous photo is again included to show you the snow. That's me crossing a pretty large snowfield as we continue to hike from Mt. Hokkaidake to Mt. Hakuundake. The snow here was relatively soft and this snowfield was not dangerous to cross for that reason and also for the reason that the slope was not very significant, so there was very little concern that we were going to lose our footing and go careening down the slope and be injured.

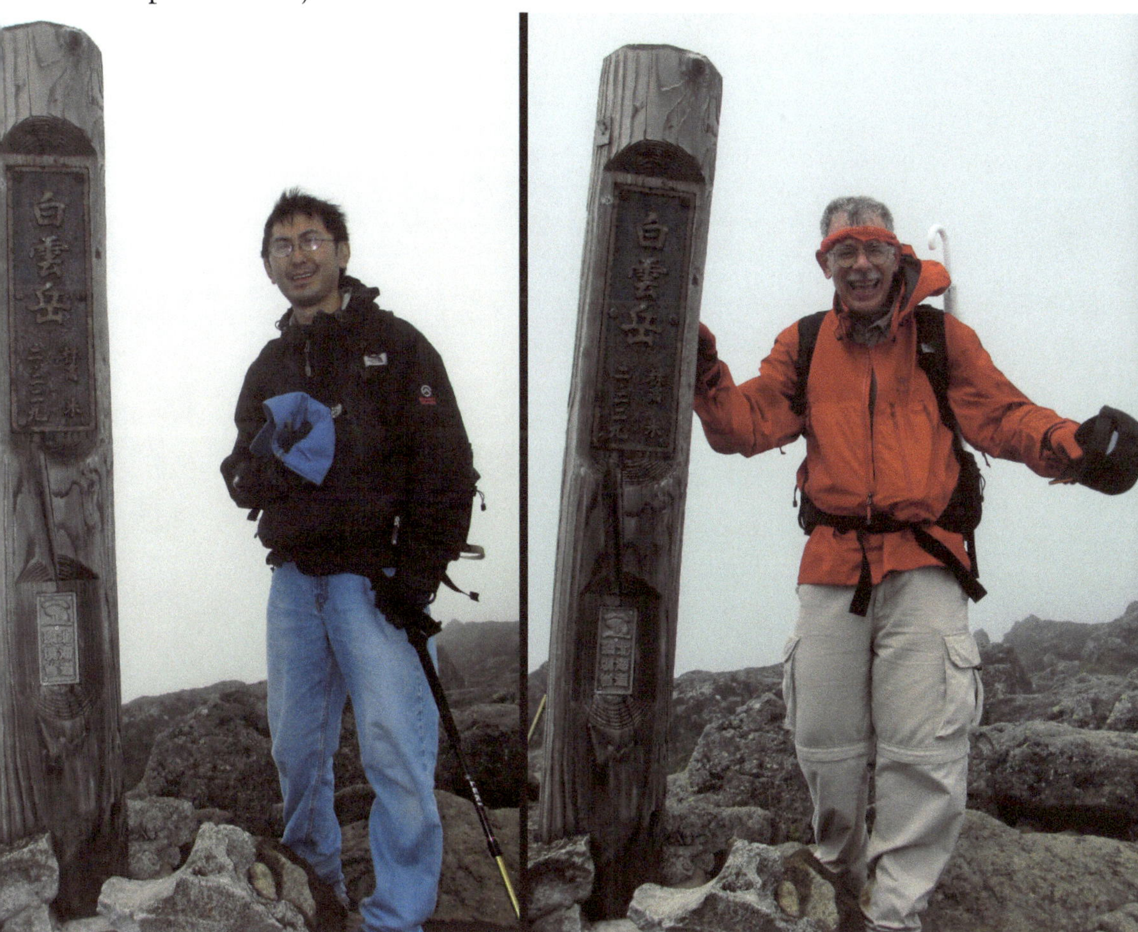

The image immediately above shows Kazuya and me at the summit of Mt. Hakuundake (2,230 m = 7,315 ft). This was on August 8, 2010 at 12:20 PM. You can probably again deduce from the photos, that the wind is still blowing very hard, as we both are holding our caps in our hands, you can see that Kazuya's hair is blowing around and that my jacket hood is blowing around. It also is not very warm, the chill factor with the wind is making the real feel quite cold – cold enough so that we are both wearing gloves.

If you once again go back to the map on Page 14 you will note that we have come quite a distance from the Mt. Kurodake Hut. We crossed over the summit of Mt. Hokkaidake and at that point we were probably a little less than one-half of the distance from the Mt. Kurodake Hut to Mt. Hakuundake. Then we continued on to here. Now we have to head back to the Mt. Kurodake Hut, as we'll stay there again tonight. So, we will again cross over the summit of Mt. Hokkaidake and then again cross the stream flowing out of "Poison Hot Spring Valley".

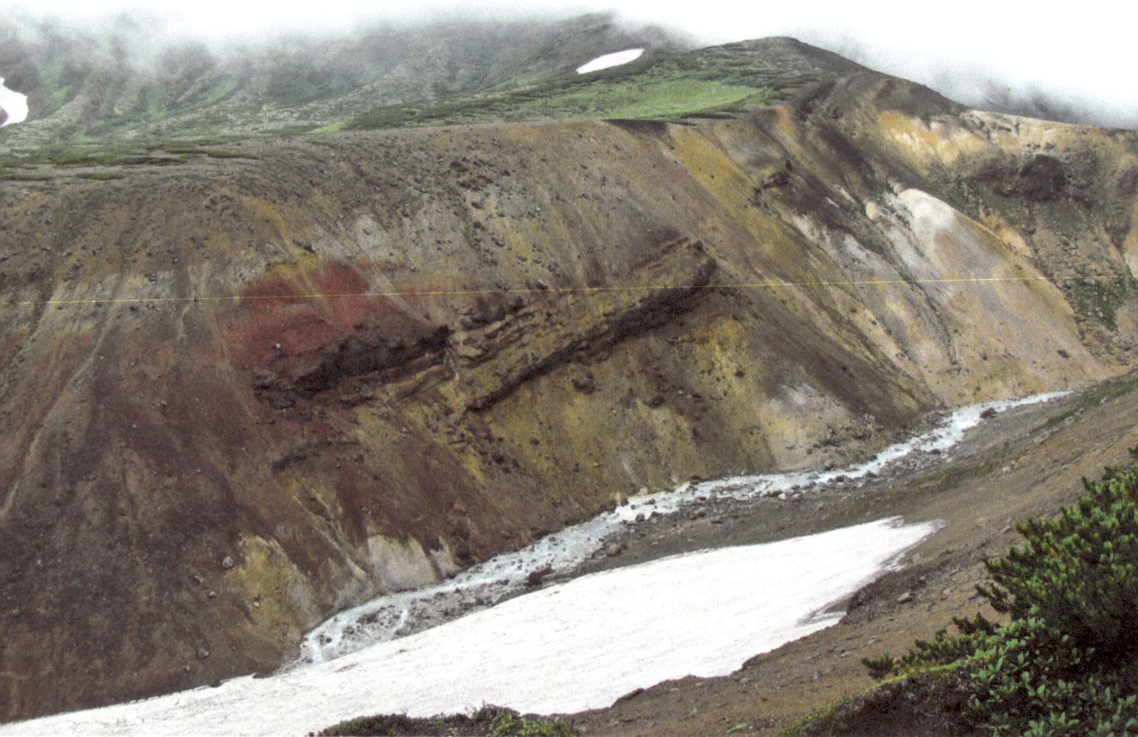

The photo immediately above was taken the following day – August 9th – as we hiked from the Mt. Kurodake Hut towards Mt. Hokuchindake (2,244 meters = 7,362 ft). It shows the stream which flows out of "Poison Hot Spring Valley". This is the stream which we had to cross yesterday on our hike to and climb of Ht. Hokkaidake. You may note that although the weather is still extremely cloudy, that at least it is somewhat bright, and in addition, it is not presently raining. Note the colors in the rock slope across the valley and also note the snowdrift remaining just a ways below us.

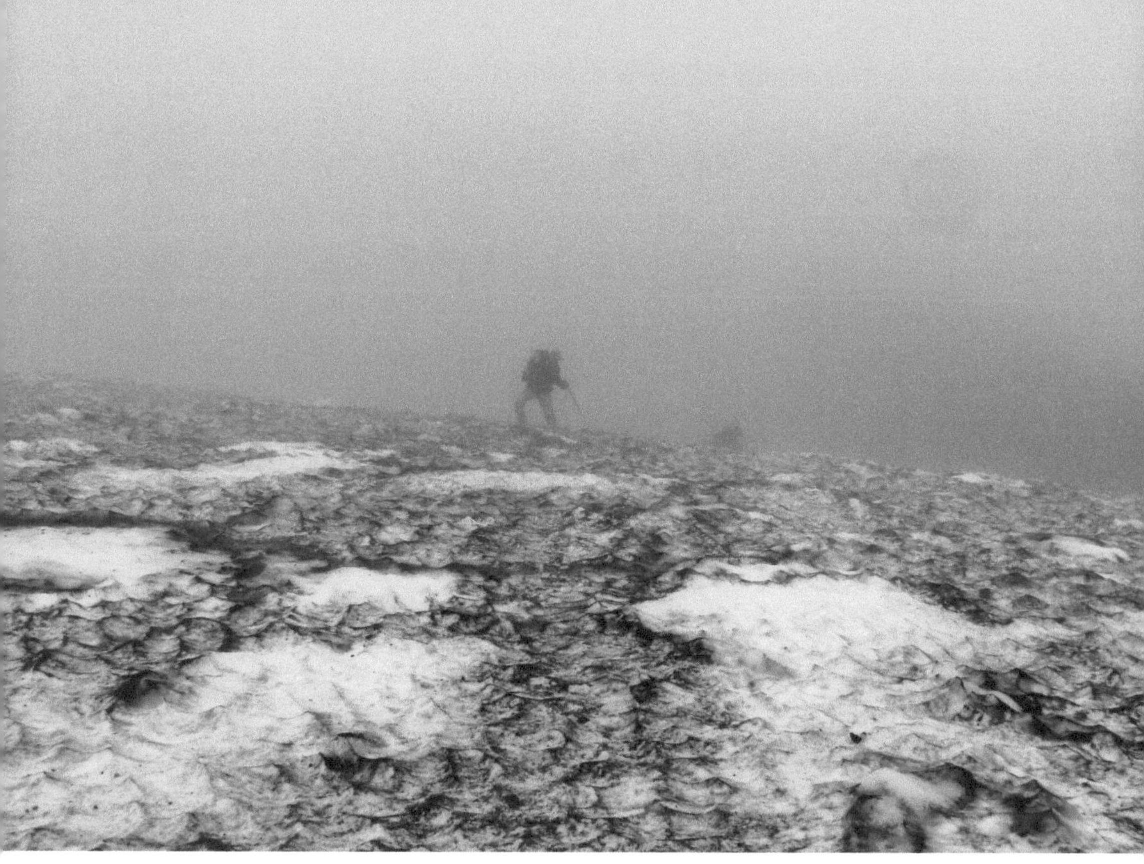

The above photo – in near whiteout conditions – was also taken on the trail to Mt. Hokuchindake. We had to cross an extremely dangerous snowfield that was on a steep slope – if we had lost our footing we would have had no way to stop. We did not have crampons with us so we just had to try and dig in with our boot soles as best we could. We had a third person following us up and across this snowfield and he was really scared and asked us to make sure that he got to the top of it alive, so we waited for him as we went. This photo shows Kazuya and the third person. We were in the clouds, so there was no visible trail and it was questionable which direction to go. I led and assumed we had to go uphill (according to the map) and I finally saw yellow paint marks on the rocks ahead – that is how they mark the trails here — WHEW!!

The next photo (on the following page) shows both Kazuya and me at the summit of Mt. Hokuchindake (2,244 meters = 7,362 ft). This was one of the few times on this adventure when there were more than just the two of us at the summit of a mountain. The person who took this photo for us was the same one who asked us to be sure that he got up and across the snowfield alive. You may recall the previous mention that Mt. Hokuchindake is the second highest peak on Hokkaido. We were sure that the view from this summit could have been really fine, but when we were here we could not see a thing beyond 200 meters or so in front of us. We spent thirty or forty minutes here hoping that the clouds would part so that we could see something, but it just did not happen. Oh well, maybe we can return here again at some point in the future and see what it looks like on a sunny day.

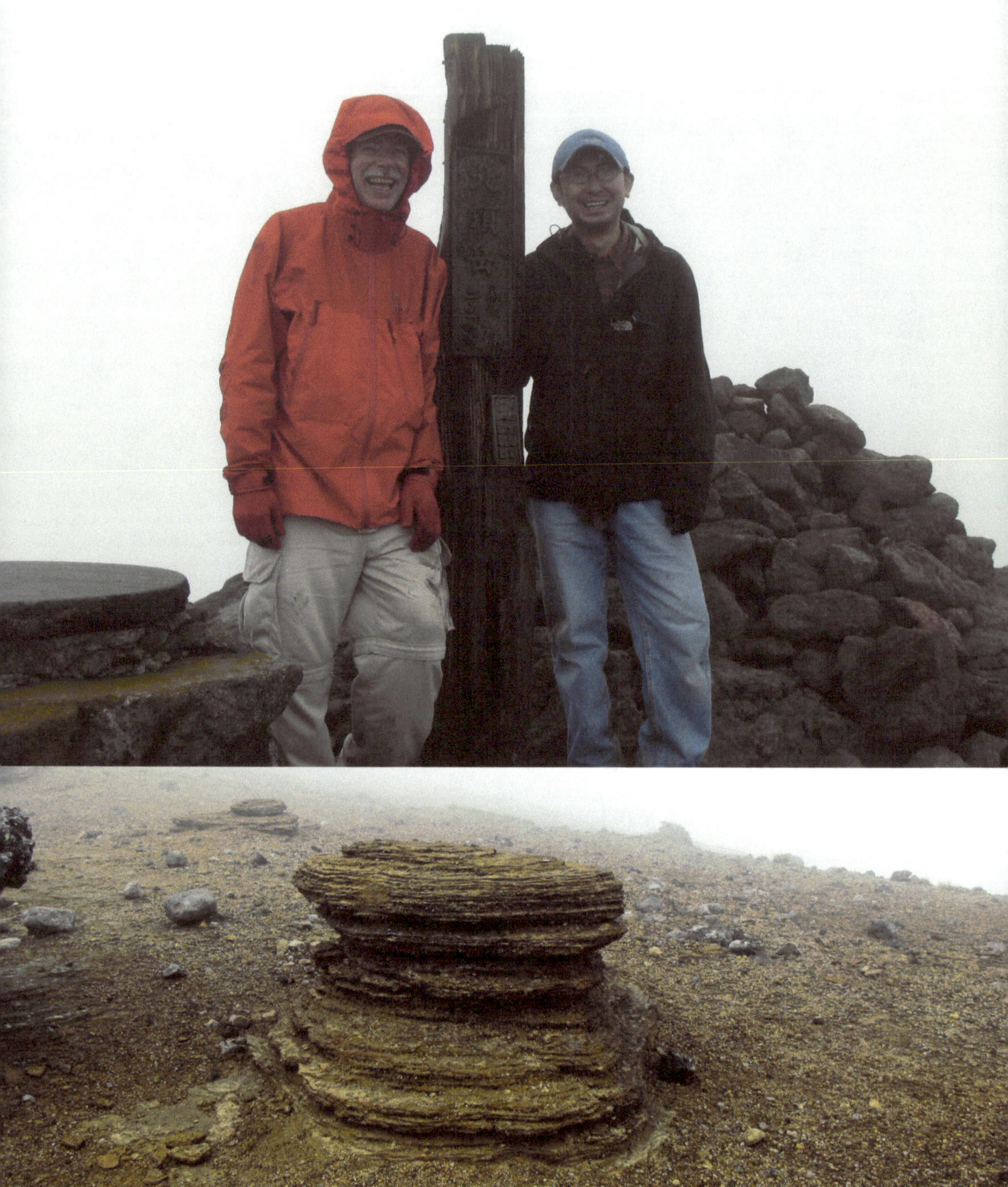

The previous photo, at the bottom of the facing page, shows some kind of rock artifact which we passed as we descended Mt. Hokuchindake. Obviously this is an area of sedimentary deposits. You can see a smaller, but similar piece behind and to the left of this one. We found several interesting artifacts on this adventure, but this was one of the more intriguing ones.

We have referred to "Poison Hot Spring Valley" already and told you that there is supposedly a poison hot spring here and that's why we refer to it as "Poison Hot Spring Valley". There are trails on all of the ridges which surround this valley. When the wind blows up out of the valley you can smell a very strong odor of sulfur. Mt. Hokkaidake is on the southeast side of this valley, Mt. Hokuchindake is on the northwest side of the valley, while Mt. Araidake and Mt. Mamiyadake are at the head of the valley. As you can see in the photo on this page, there is very little vegetation growing in this valley. The second time we were here, we could even see an area which appeared to have been burned. We assumed that was due to an eruption of extremely hot or poisonous water from the hot spring.

It is a very intriguing valley and despite its large size and the relative openness of the area we have never noted a bear or other large animal crossing it. We have seen bears in other areas of this National Park, both in 2009 and again in 2010, but nothing in "Poison Hot Spring Valley". Personally I have to wonder if it is as dangerous as they want people to believe – I want to go into this valley and see it for myself.

The outlined area in this photo shows the approximate area shown in the upper photo on the following page.

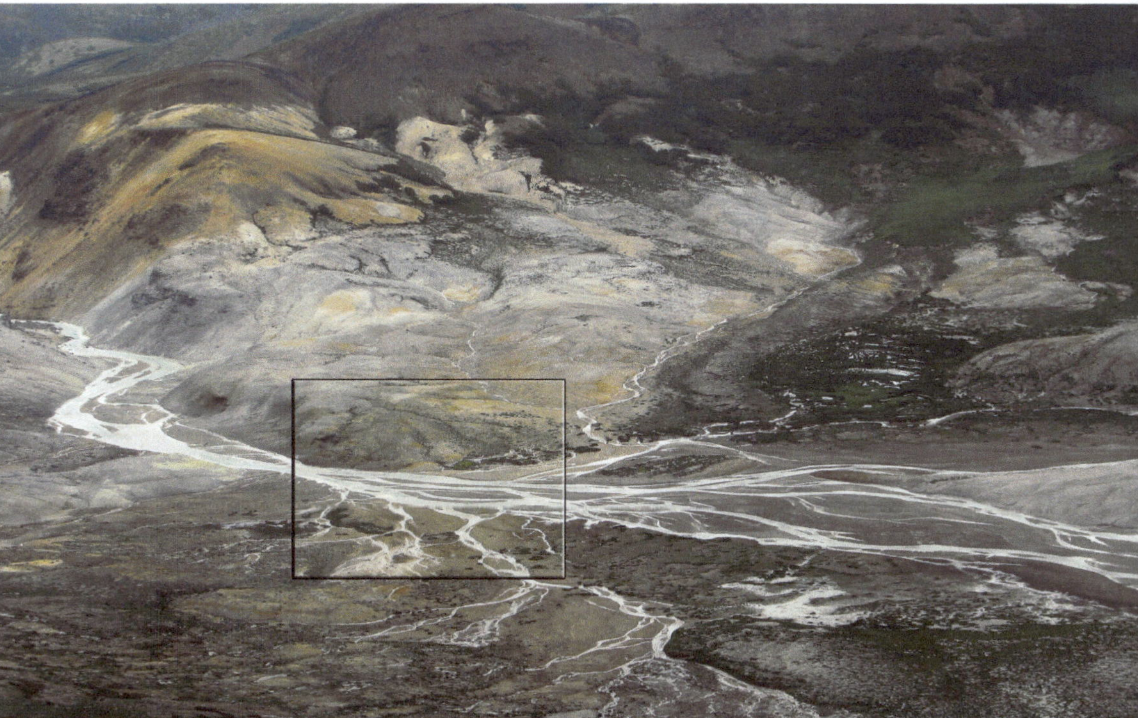

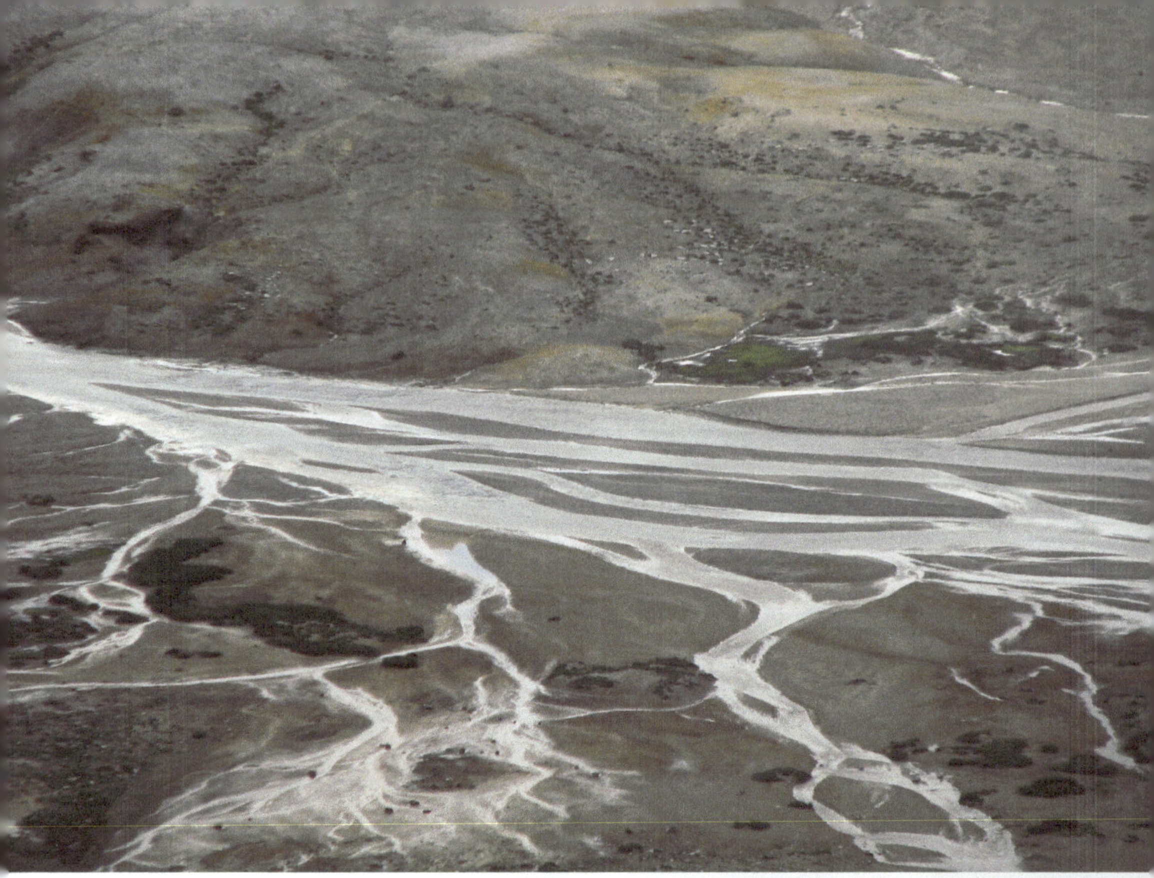

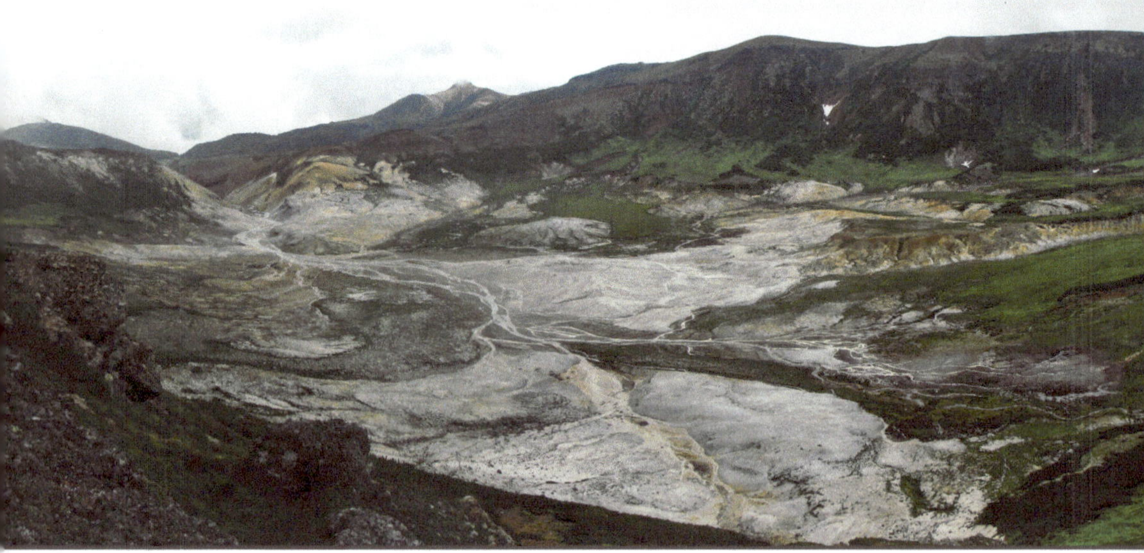

The photo immediately above shows the majority of what we refer to as "Poison Hot Spring Valley". The highest mountain, just to the right of the center of the photo is Mt. Hokkaidake. The valley to the left of center shows the approximate area of the photo on page 22. You will probably agree that this looks like a very interesting valley. Would you like to step foot into that valley as much as I would?

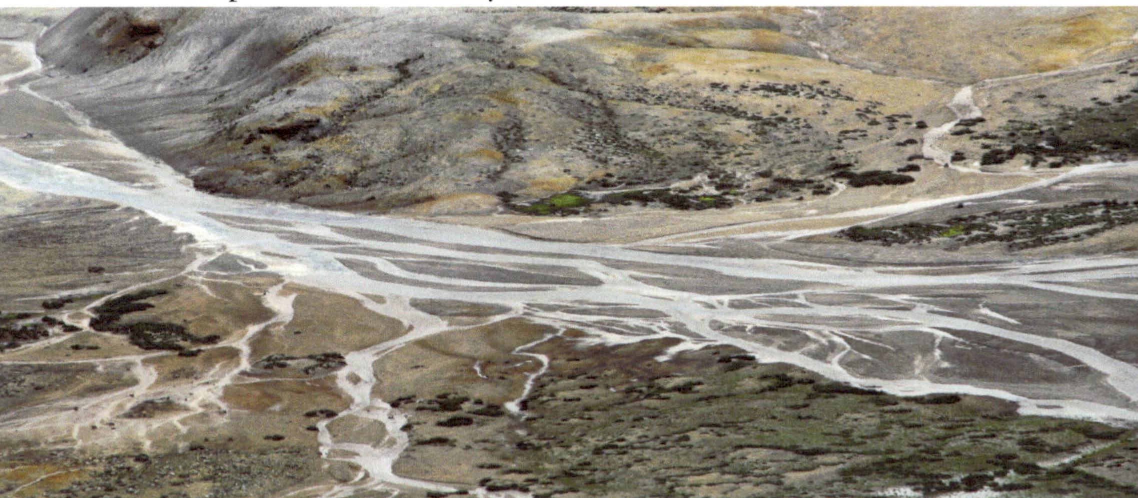

The photo just above is another of "Poison Hot Spring Valley". Don't you have to wonder why so very little vegetation grows down there? In addition, also note that what little vegetation there is, appears to be so stunted – there are no trees at all, the tallest things there are a few scraggly looking bushes.

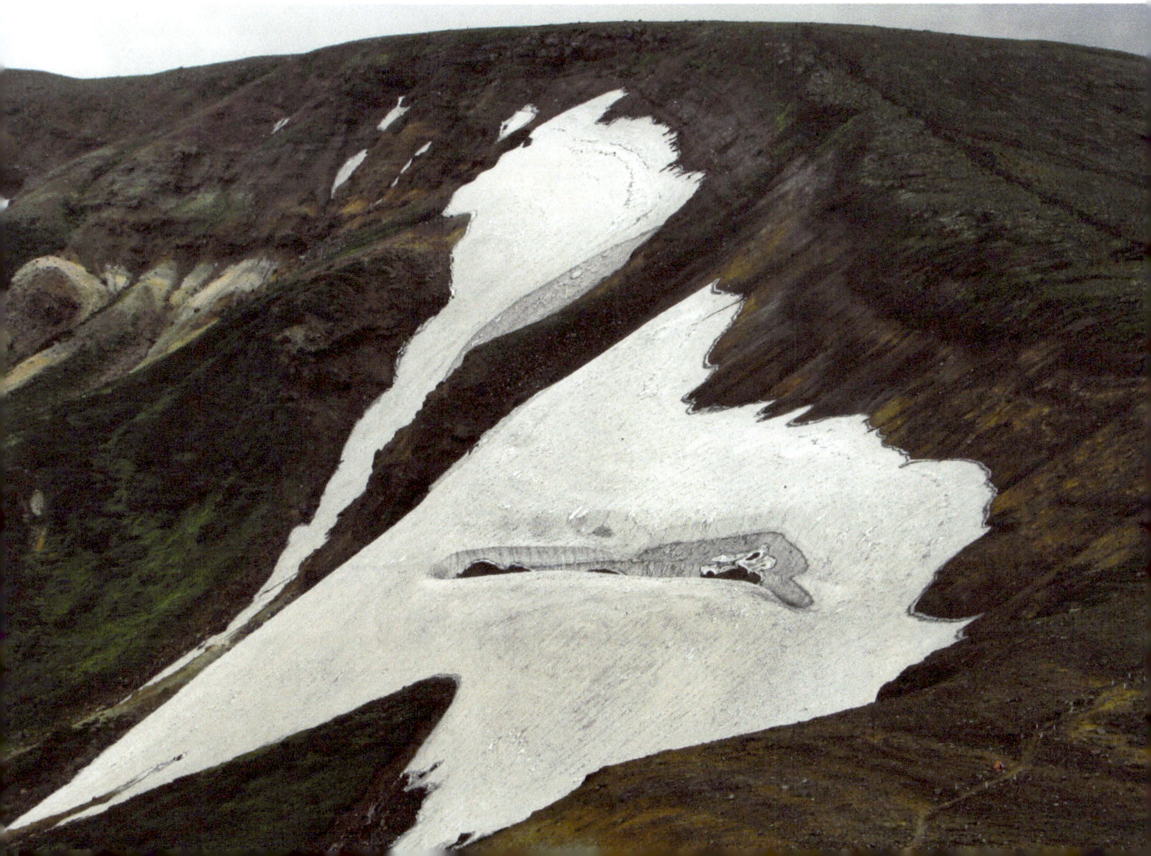

The lower photo on the previous page shows a very large snowdrift. This was taken right at the wall which marks the western edge of "Poison Hot Spring Valley". If you go back and look at the map again, this would be just about below Mt. Nakadake, or possibly between Mt. Nakadake and the trail which heads off towards Nakadake Hot Spring.

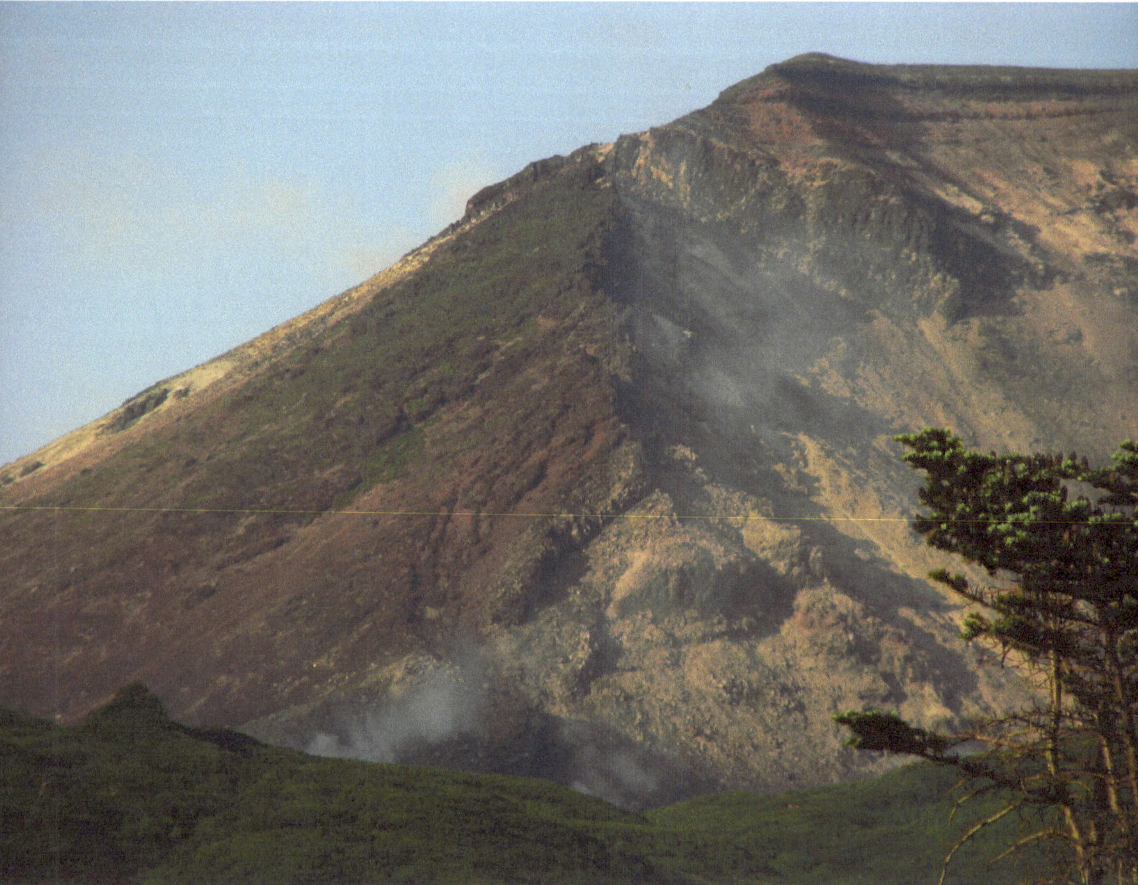

The photo immediately above shows just a portion of Mt. Asahidake, from the bottom of the Ropeway. This photo was taken in 2009, the year we were here and the weather was more sunny than cloudy.

Notice the smoke coming up behind the green hill – it is not a forest fire – that smoke is coming from the active volcanic fumaroles on this mountain.

Most of the remaining photos of this mountain were taken during 2009, when the weather was nice, so you can look forward to more sunny photos.

The next photo shows Mt. Asahidake (2,291 meters = 7,516 feet) as the sun rises over the top of it. It was 6:11 AM when this photo was taken and the place was along the trail as we hiked from the top of the

Asahidake ropeway up towards Sugatami Pond. In a little less than three hours, we will be at the summit of this mountain. As mentioned earlier, Mt. Asahidake is the highest mountain on Hokkaido.

The vertical panoramic image on the following page was taken from the scenic overlook at Sugatami Pond as one begins the ascent of Mt. Asahidake. This is the first photo which really shows you that this is an active volcano. The steam fumaroles are very evident here. You can also see the shoulder of Mt. Asahidake in this image.

When we arrived at this point we were so very amazed at just how much smoke or steam is pouring out of the ground here and this image, thanks to the reflection in Sugatami Pond makes it look double the amount that it actually is. We'll show you some additional photos with smoke in them, some from up quite higher on Mt. Asahidake. We hope that you can be patient and that you'll also enjoy looking at the amazing power of nature.

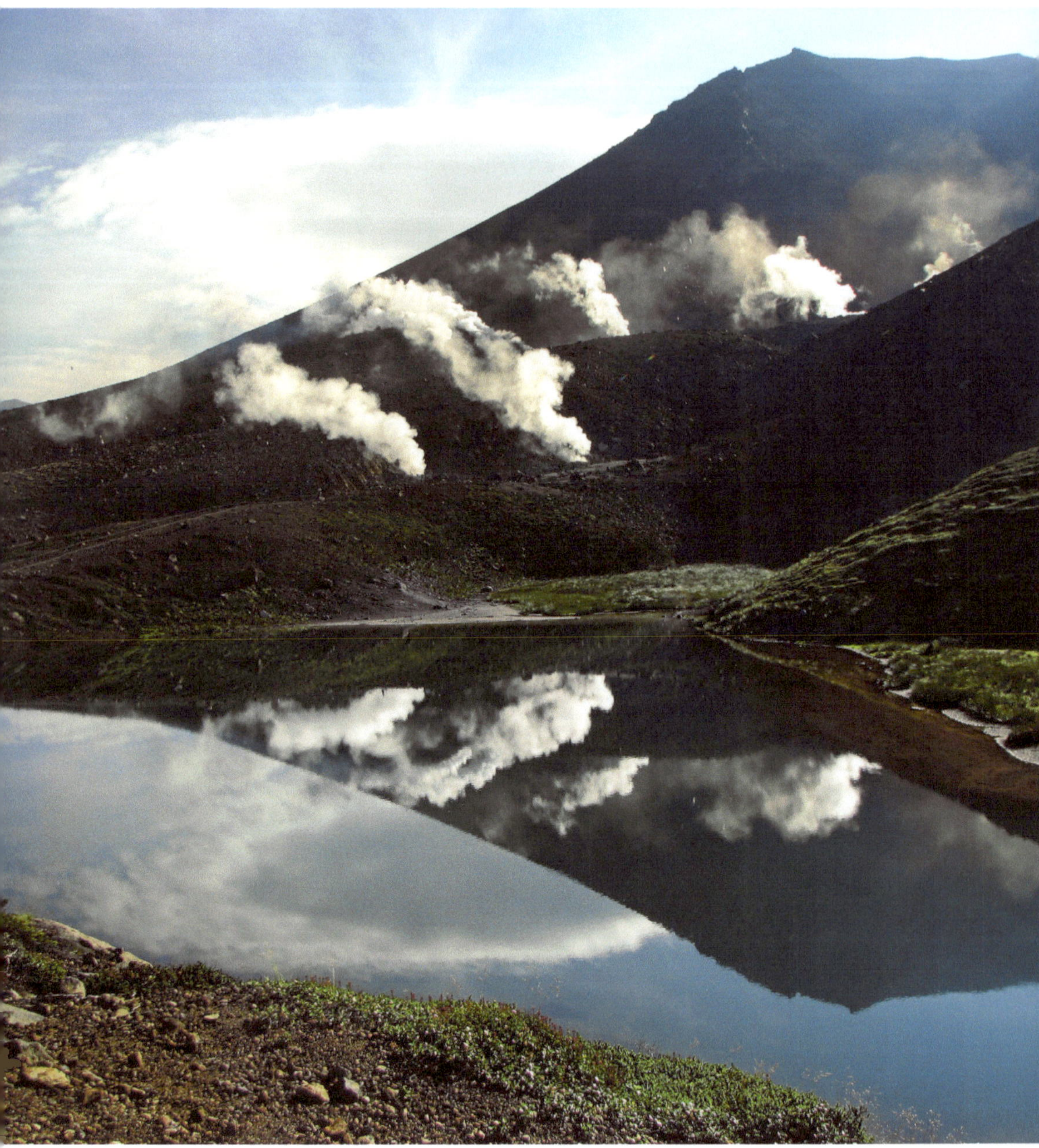

In the following photo you can once again get a feeling of the power of nature, and if you examine the lower edge of the photo, near the left side, you can find two people silhouetted against the steam and also get a feeling for the scale of things here. This photo was actually taken from a different trail than the one just above, so although the angle looks quite similar it is more different than it appears to be. The lighting of this photo is quite interesting – this side of Mt. Asahidake is shaded, but the steam is very well lighted by the sun. It was actually quite difficult lighting conditions for photography.

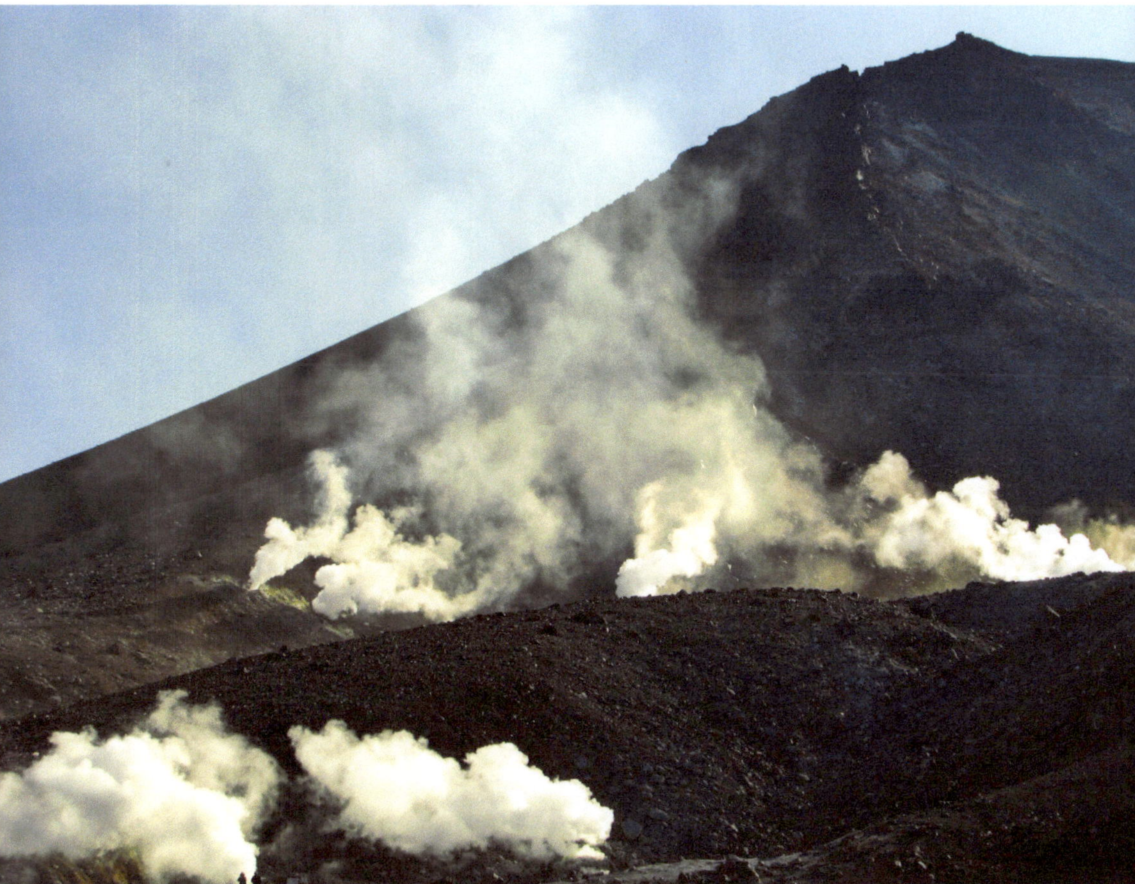

The upper photo on the next page really gives you a sense of the scale of things – the people are so small in relation to the steam coming up behind them. This photo was taken along the same trail as the photo on this page, but from a different vantage point.

The lower photo on the following page features the emergency shelter at Sugatami Pond. It looks very sturdy, wouldn't you agree? There is a warning sign here stating that this shelter does not have a toilet – ha! With the lighting and the colors of the rock used to construct this hut it really makes it especially photogenic.

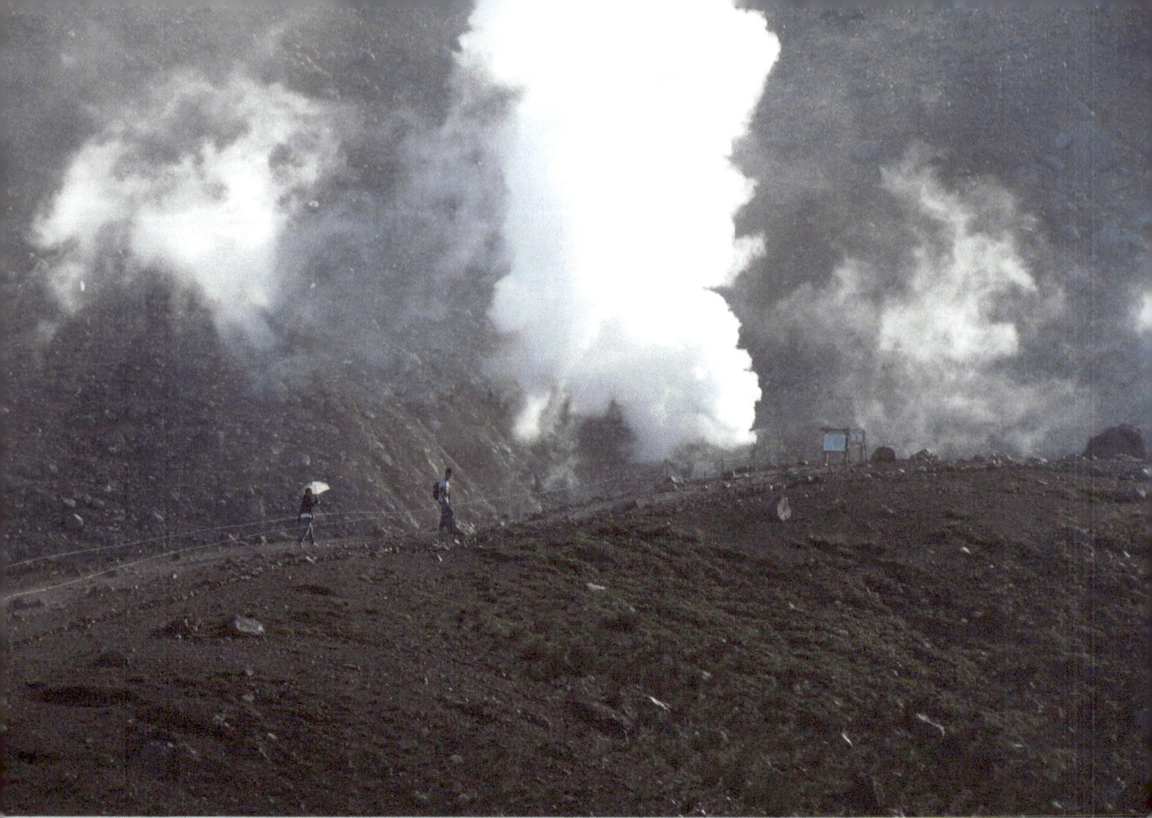

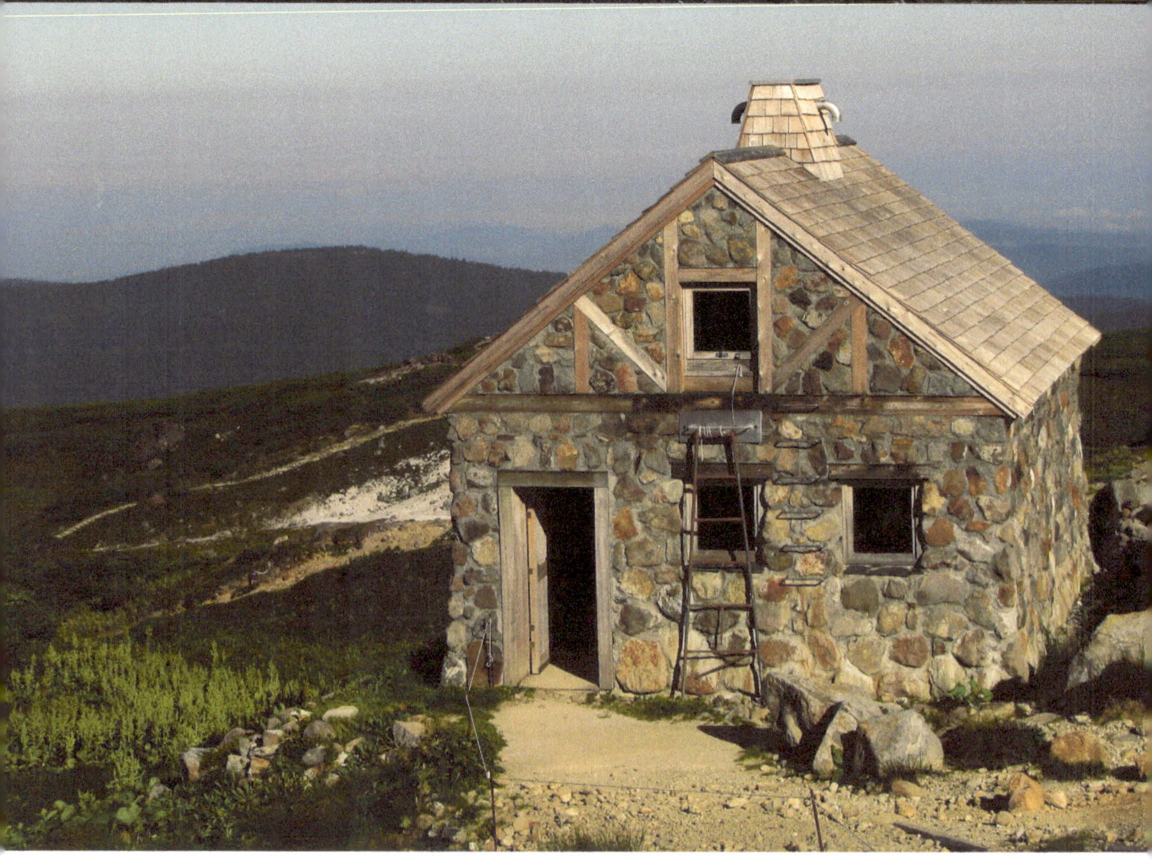

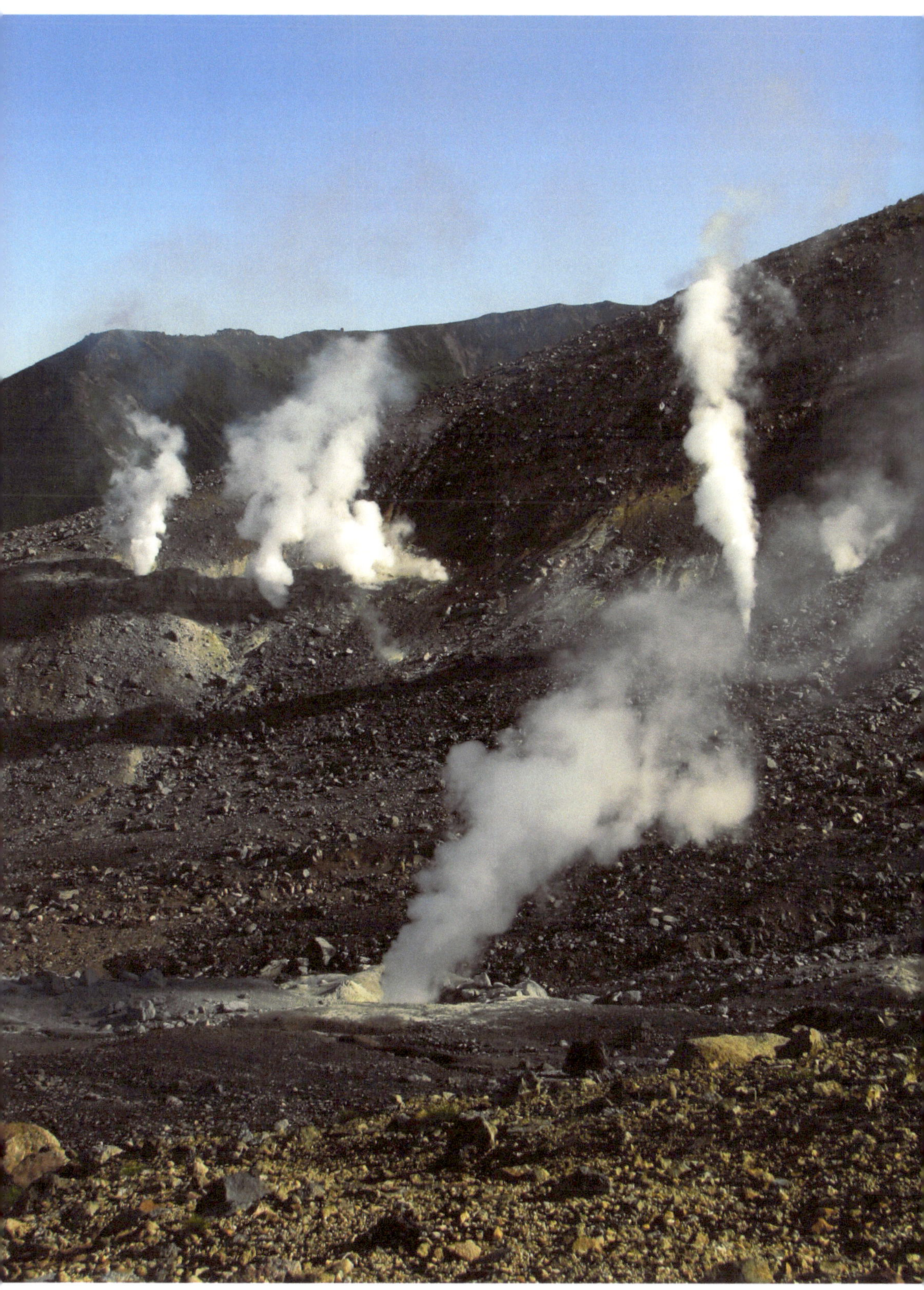

The photo on the previous page is really amazing in the early morning light. The time was 7:23 AM and as you know from the photo on page 29, the sun just came over the top of the mountain a little over an hour ago. That is what gives these steam geysers their long shadows and probably also why there is no breeze and the steam is going pretty much straight up.

The photo on this page was taken from quite a bit higher on Mt. Asahidake and shows you this valley where all of these fumaroles are located. Near the left edge of the photo you can see the building which houses the machinery for the ropeway. In addition to this you can also see a portion of Sugatami Pond on the left edge of the photo.

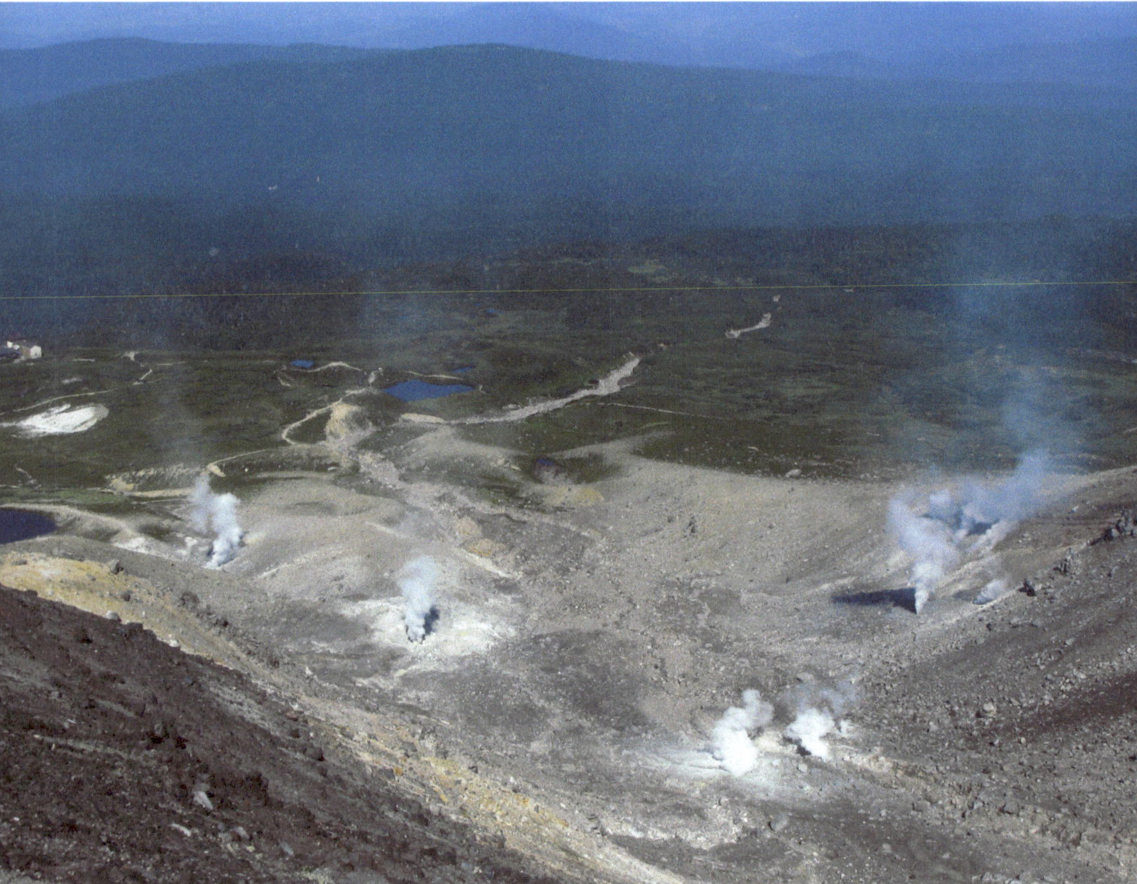

The photo on the facing page shows a close-up of one of these steam vents or fumaroles on the side of the mountain. No, we did not get this close to one of these things, this shot was taken with a zoom lens from quite a distance away. This shot gives a better indication of the size of these vents and it also shows the accumulation of sulfur (the yellow deposit on the rocks). Wonder what the temperature of the steam is?

Wonder how close one would have to approach before one started to feel the heat – assuming that the steam was rising straight up at the time?

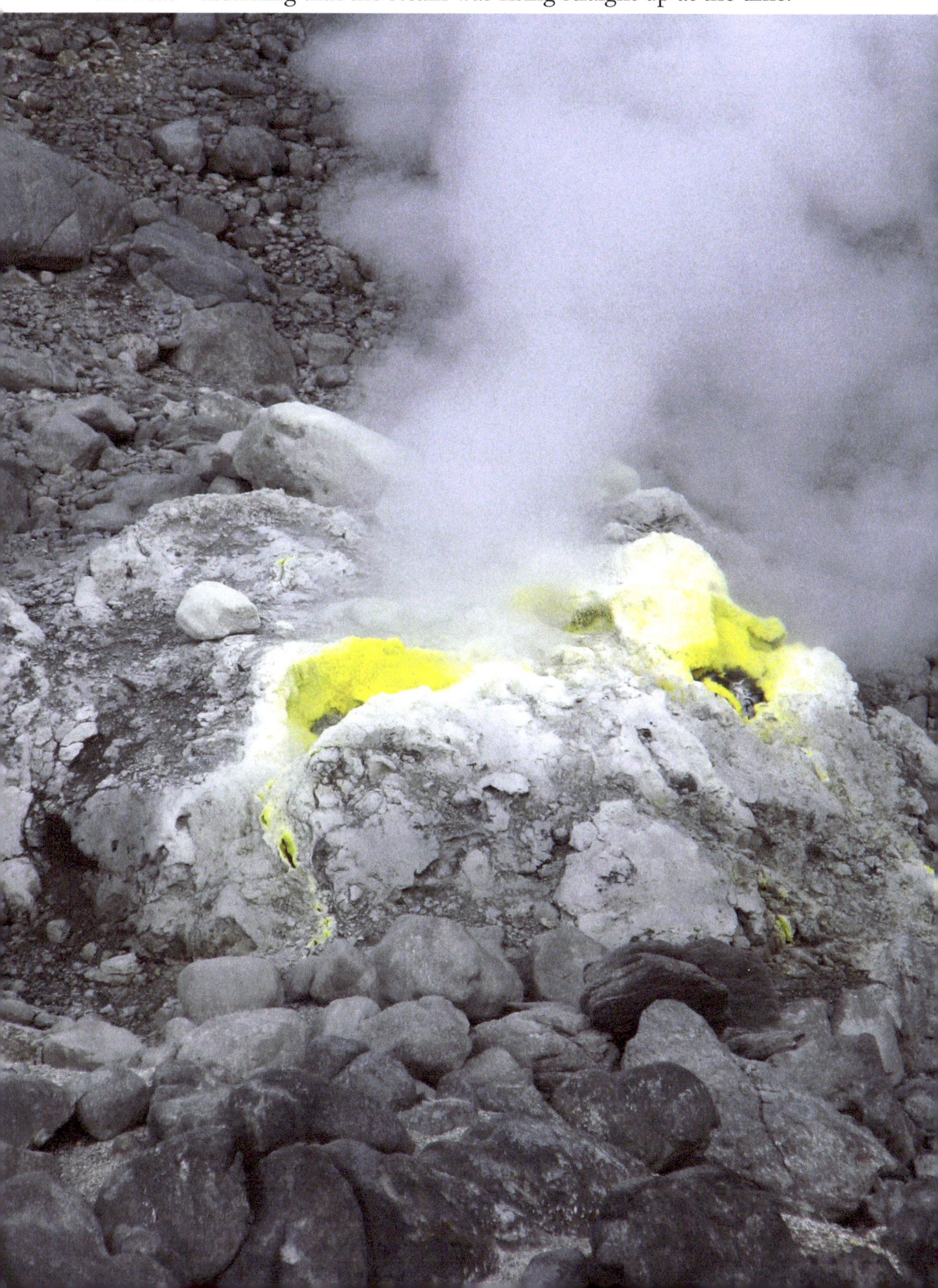

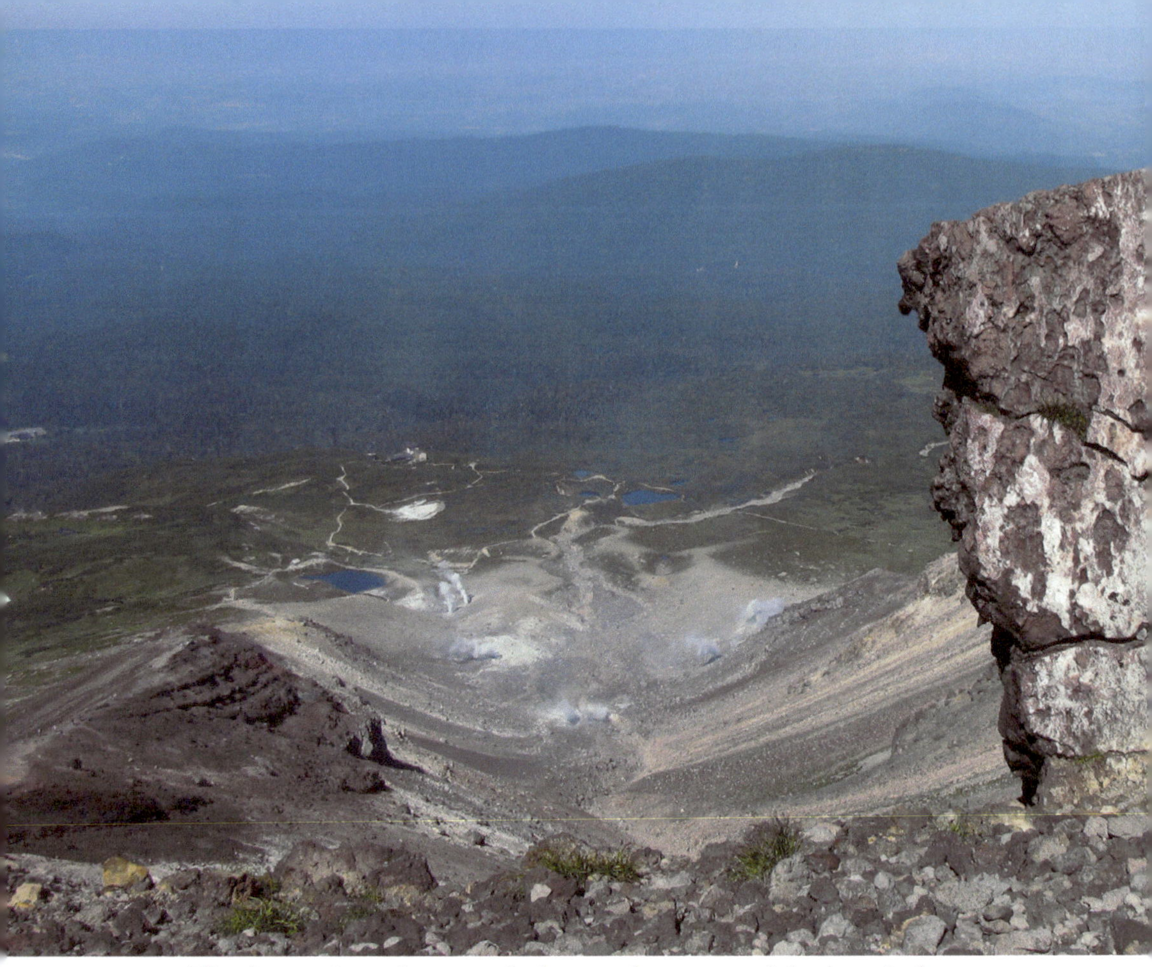

The image just above and also to the upper right is a 2-shot pano-ramic image that shows a volcanic artifact which is quite close to the sum-mit of Mt. Asahidake. It is called "safe rock", most likely because of its re-semblance to a huge vault – it is just a huge rock cube sitting here on the edge of the mountain. It is difficult to know the precise location where this photo was taken from, but you are looking at the entire rock here – part of it on this page and part of it on page 37. In the portion of the image shown on this page you can see the volcanic valley as well as Sugatami Pond, the top of the ropeway and even the very photogenic emergency shelter near Sugatami Pond if you study it closely enough.

In the portion of the image on the facing page, to the right of "safe rock" is a shoulder of Mt. Asahidake – as you can surmise – we are now quite close to the summit, but before we get there, let us show you one more photo (lower photo – facing page) looking more or less to the east. This is most likely Mount Ushiro-Asahidake (後旭岳) (2,216 m = 7,270 ft) (see map – east of Mt. Asahidake), although we are not 100% sure.

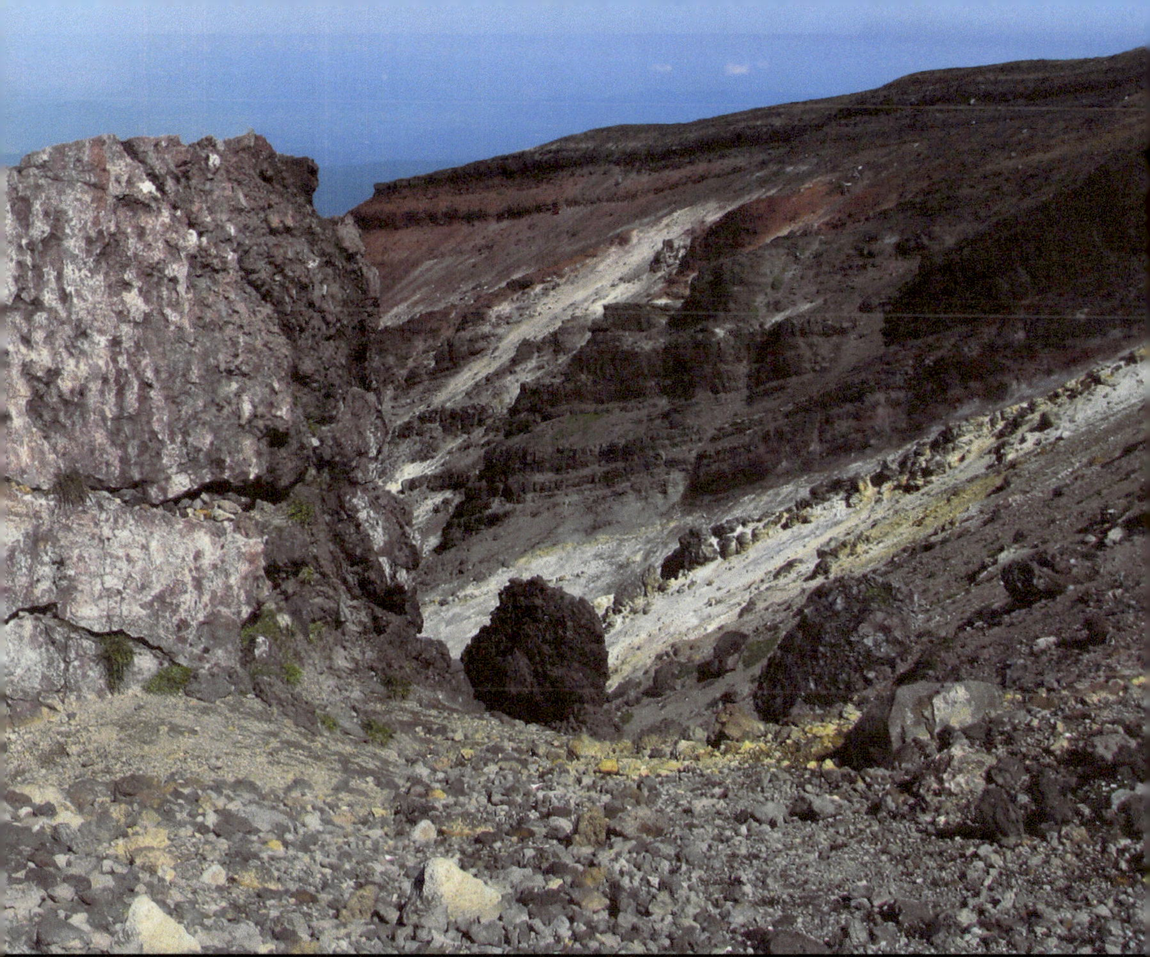

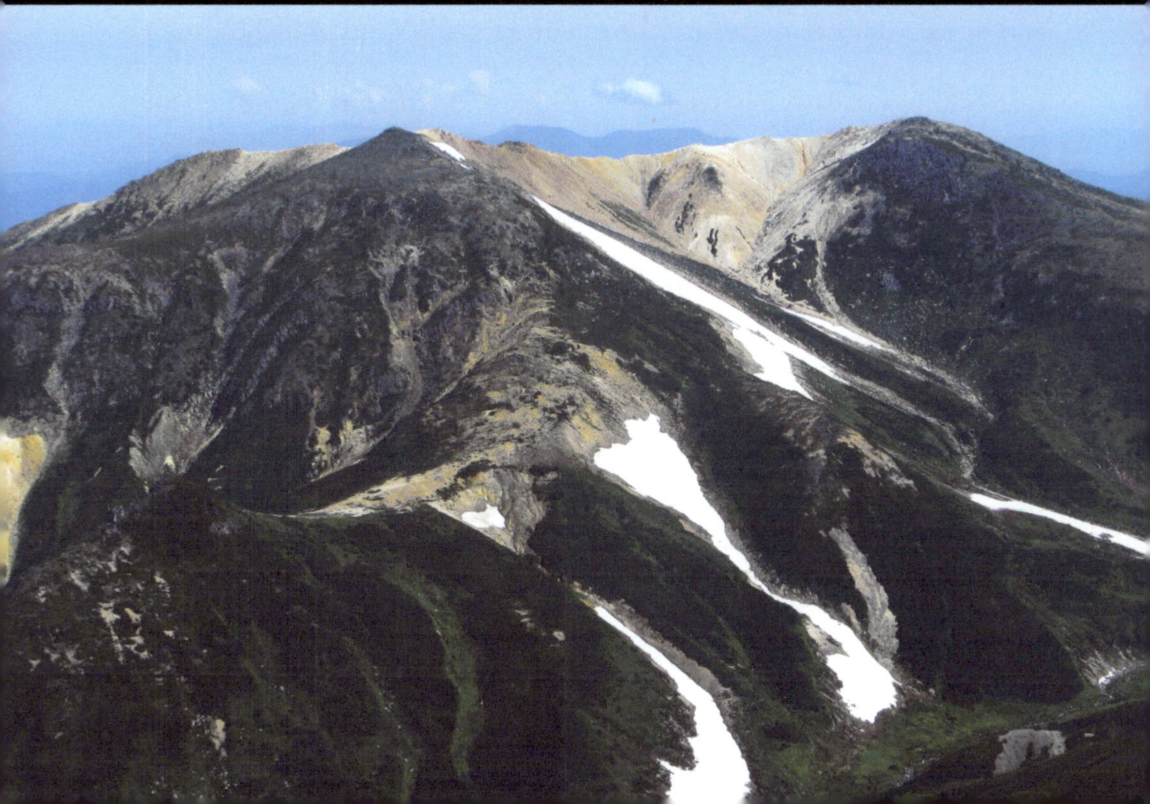

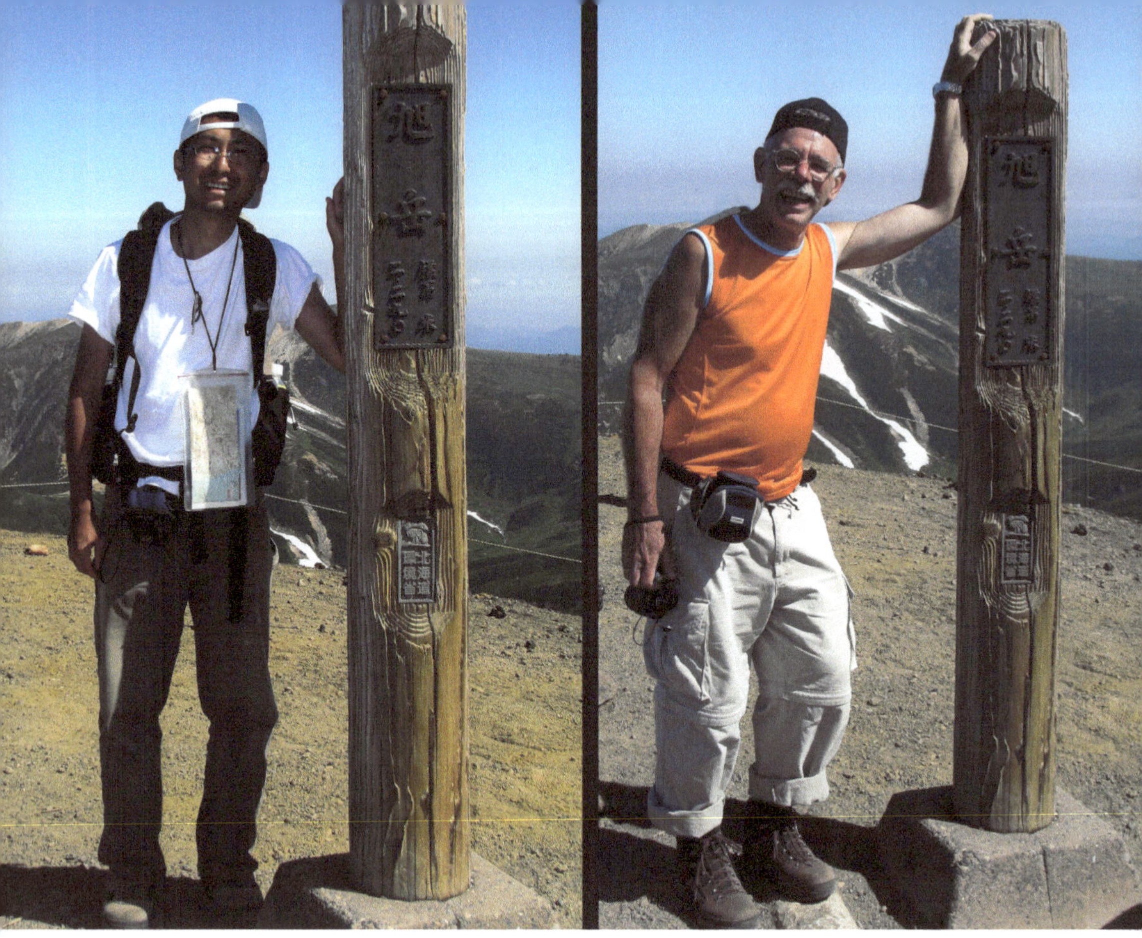

The above image once again shows two separate photos of Kazuya and of me. This time we are at the summit marker of the highest mountain on Hokkaido – Mt. Asahidake (2,291 m = 7,516 ft). You will note that once again, we are looking quite happy and satisfied. These two photos were taken when we climbed this mountain the first time, in 2009. In 2010 when we climbed this peak it was quite cloudy. We were able to see into the distance from time to time, but there was no sun.

The next two photos, on the facing page, show some scenery we could see from the summit area of Mt. Asahidake. They were both taken while looking to the north-northeast. In both photos, in the foreground on the left side, is Mt. Kumagadake (熊ヶ岳) (2,210 m = 7,250 ft) (see map, page 14). In the valley directly behind Mt. Kumagadake is the small pond which you can see on the map (page 14). The trail follows along the ridge on the right side of that valley. On the right side in the upper photo, that mountain is most likely Mt. Hokkaidake. In the lower photo the perfect cone-shaped mountain on the left side of the photo, in the background is Mt. Hokuchindake. You may recall that when we summited Mt. Hokuchindake, in 2010, we could not see a thing beyond about 200 meters away due to the cloudy conditions.

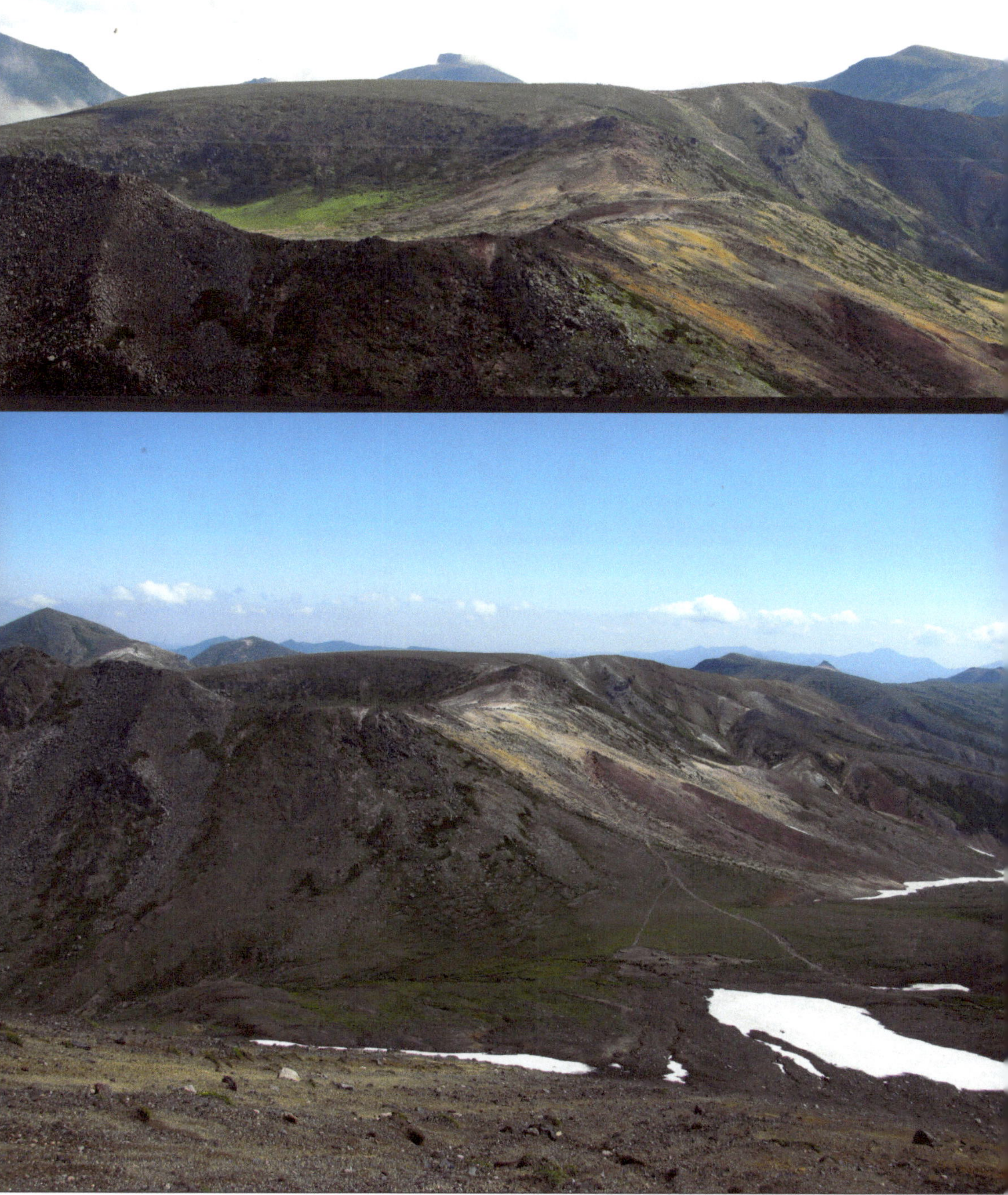

The next photo shows the backside of Mt. Asahidake and was taken

as we descended on the trail going to the northeast, towards Mt. Mamiyadake (see map). The sky is so incredibly blue in this photo that it is amazing. It was merely coincidence that we caught that person on the edge of the snowfield. It's a great way to gauge the scale of everything.

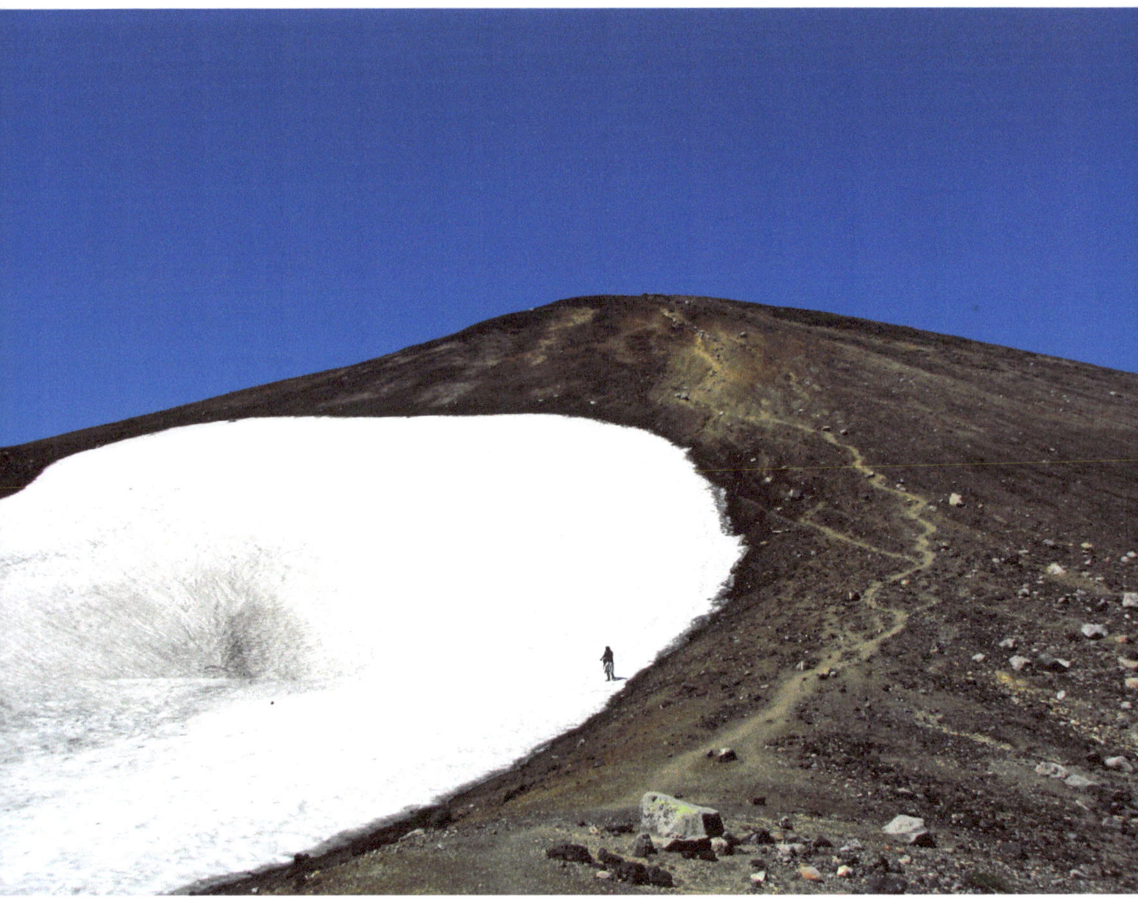

The following photo, on the facing page, was also taken as we descended Mt. Asahidake on the trail referred to just above. The mountain closest to the center is Mt. Kumagadake (熊ヶ岳) (2,210 m = 7,250 ft). We won't be summiting Mt. Kumagadake, but we will be going close to it and we'll also show you at least one photo from its opposite side.

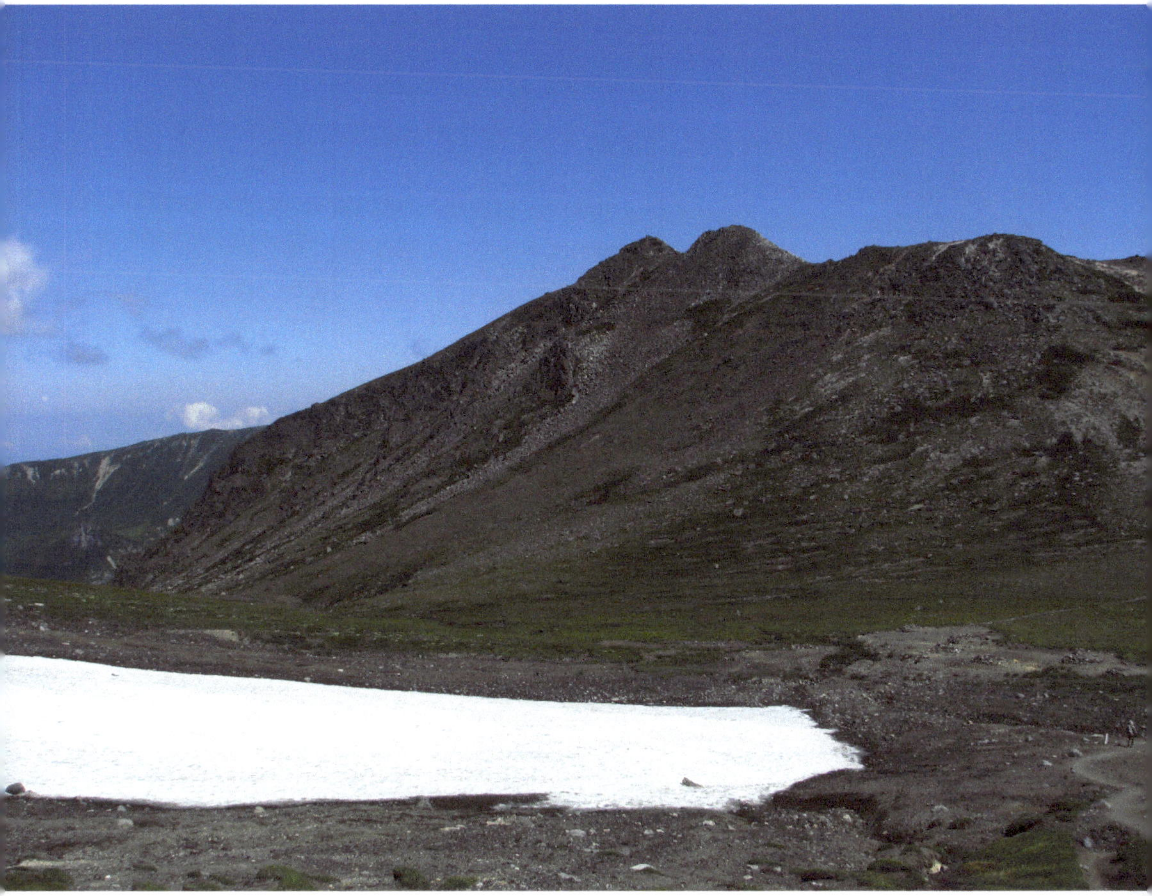

The photo just below once again shows the backside of Mt. Asahidake and the snowfields in August. It was taken from just about the lowest point in the pass between Mt. Asahidake and Mt. Kumagadake (see map on page 14).

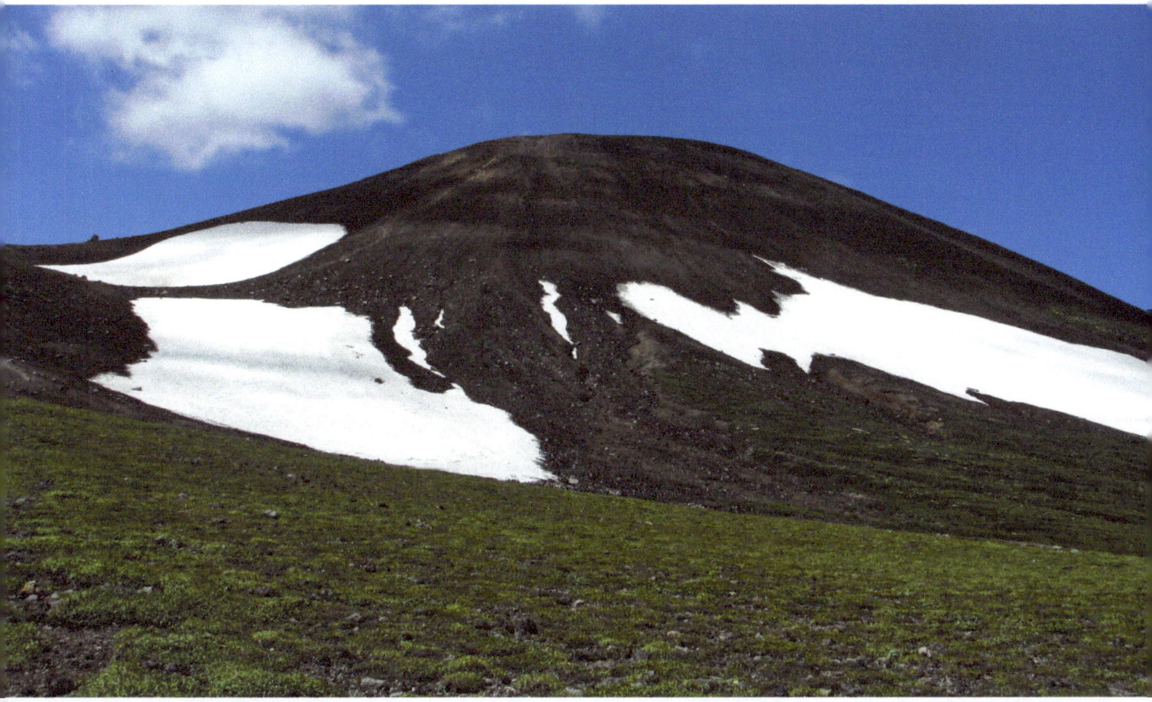

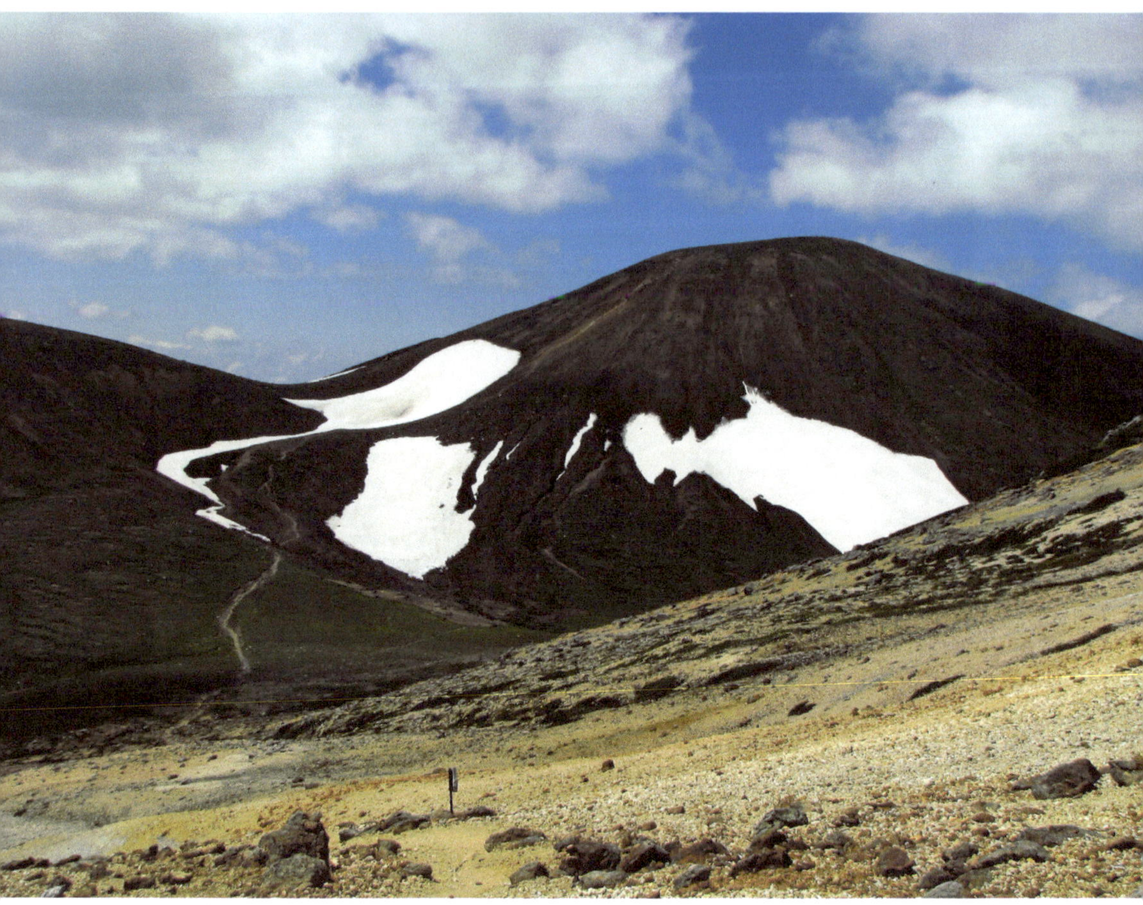

The photo immediately above is the final one you'll see of Mt. Asahidake from this side. In this photo you can see the trail as it winds its way down this side of the mountain, through the valley and up to this point. Of course that snowfield you can see near the center of the photo is the same snowfield that you saw on page 40 with the person on the edge of it for an idea of the scale of things.

Now we are working our way up the trail towards Mt. Mamiyadake and in just a short time we will be at our closest point to Mt. Kumagadake although we will not actually summit that peak.

In the photo below you can see Mt. Kumagadake (熊ヶ岳) (2,210 m = 7,250 ft) – which is that entire mountain. The person standing there is me. We have left the trail for a little while and are (on the map) still headed in the direction of Mt. Mamiyadake. We are probably about at the point a bit above the "1" in the time that says "1:30", which indicates that it takes about 1.5 hours to hike from Mt. Mamiyadake to the summit of Mt. Asahidake.

The next two photos (following page) show the crater or valley where the pond or small lake is just to the northeast of Mt. Kumagadake. In the upper photo you can appreciate the crater, the pond, Mt. Hokkaidake – the peak near the right side of the photo – and Mt. Tomadake (2,076 m = 6,811 ft).

The lower photo on the facing page once again shows the crater which lies to the northeast of Mt. Kumagadake, the pond in the crater and off in the distance is Mt. Tomadake. This photo is basically the same as the one above it except that this one is zoomed in more so that you can appreciate the barren beauty of this area to a greater extent.

Despite the remoteness of this small valley, in our two visits here we did not see any wildlife beyond a few birds. There is a nice variety of small alpine flowers here, but this book will not show you flower photos.

Now, let's continue on and keep going towards Mt. Mamiyadake.

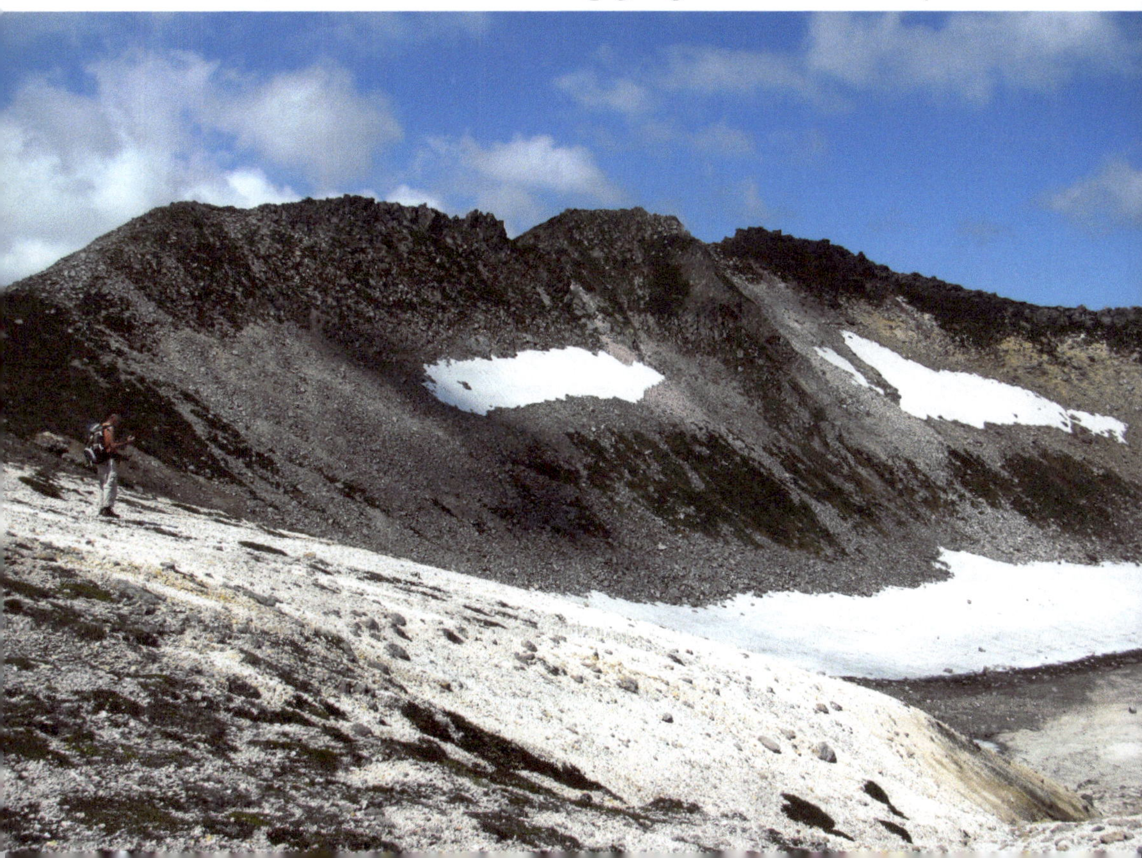

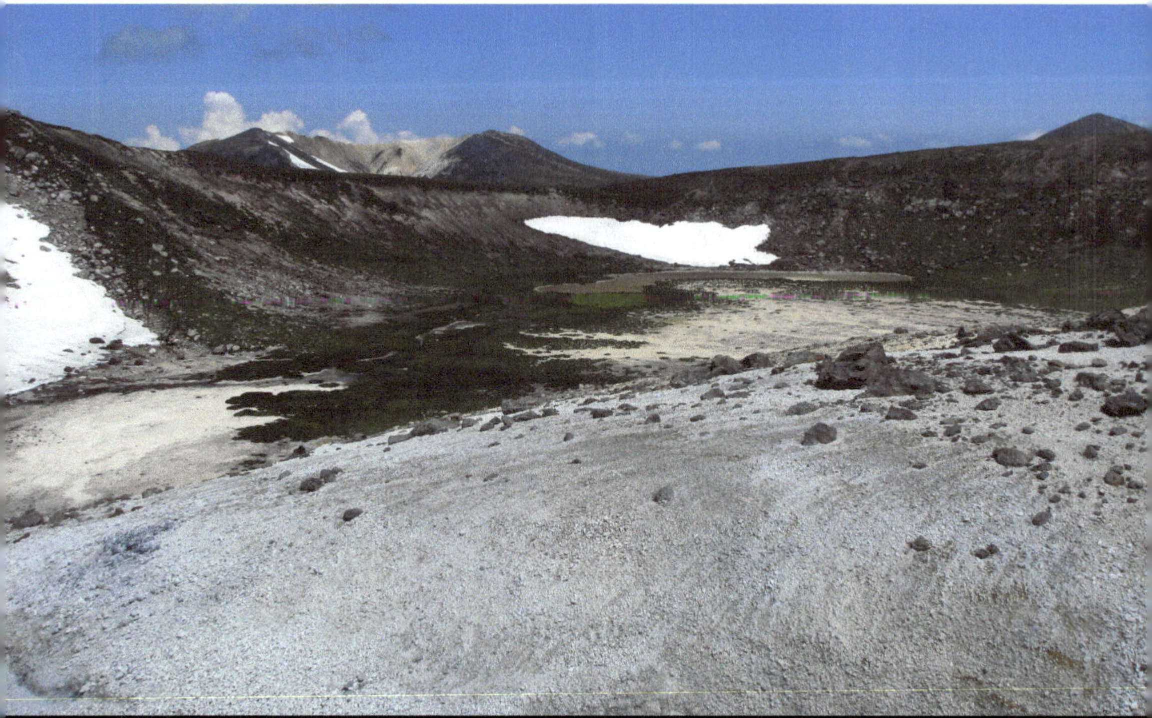

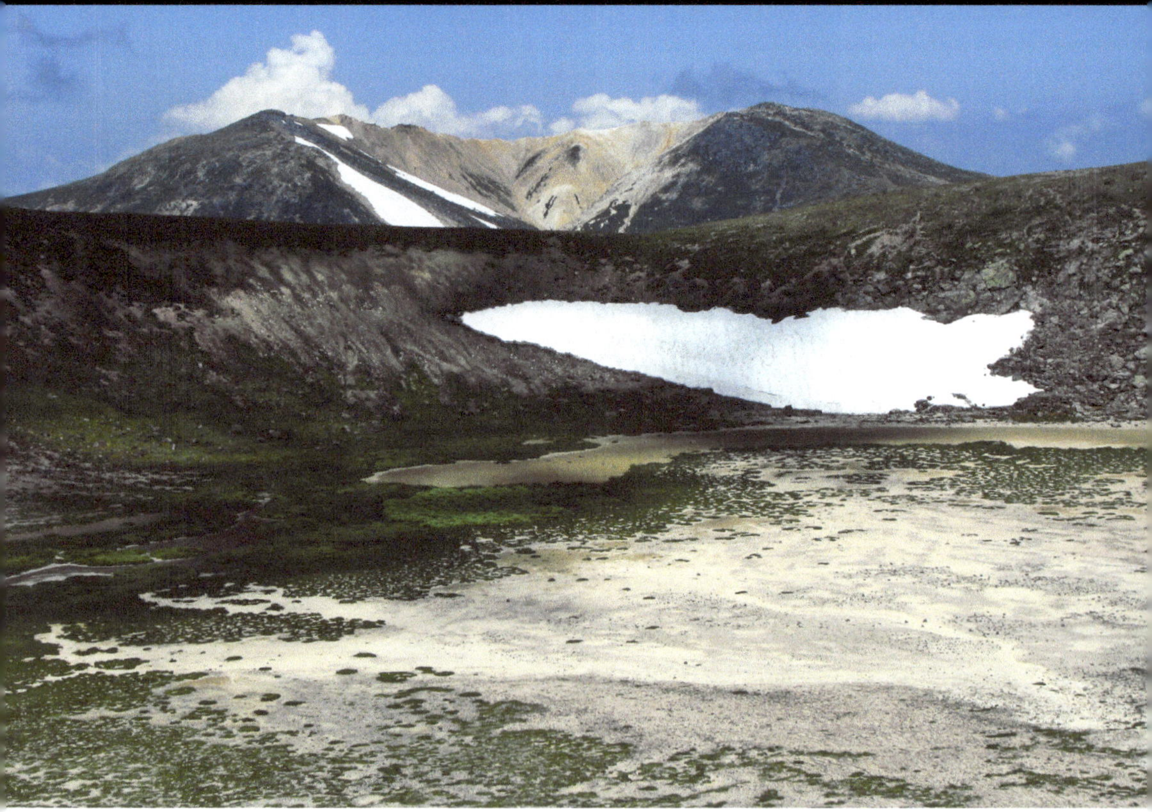

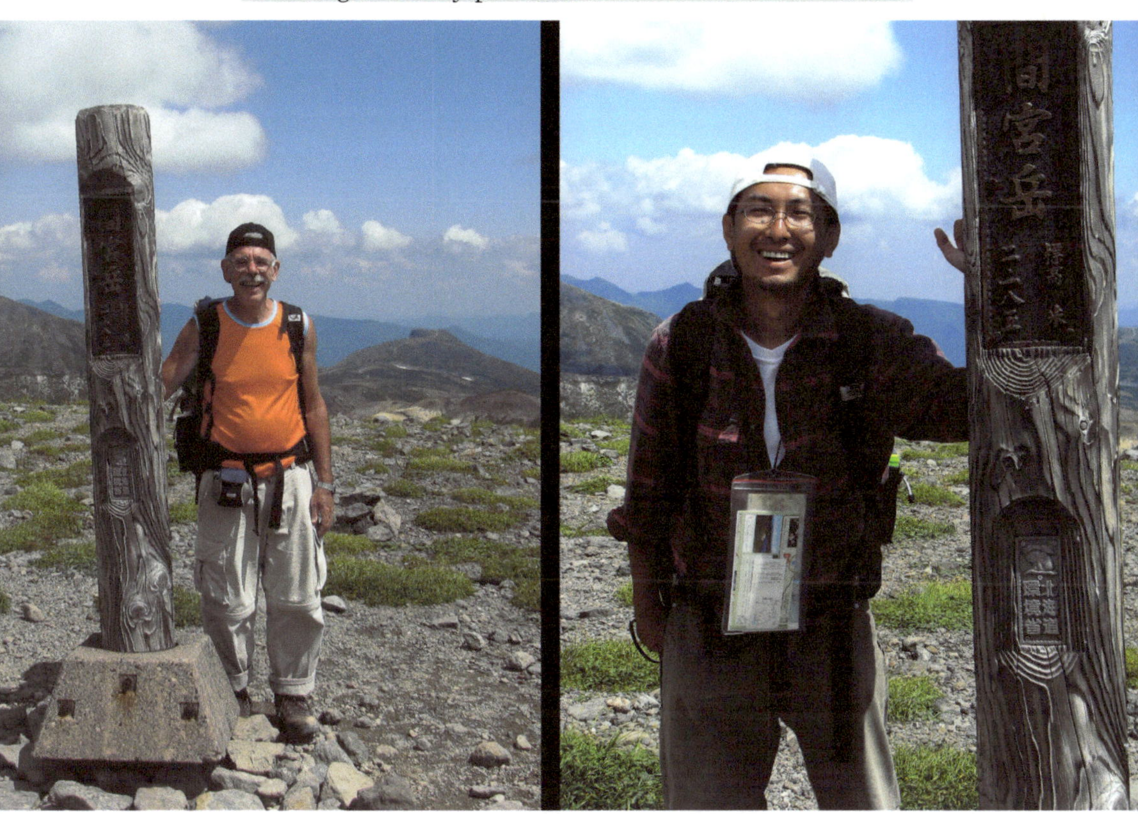

The image immediately above shows each of us at the summit of Mt. Mamiyadake (2,185 m = 7,169 ft) (see map). Have you ever seen two happier looking people? From Mt. Mamiyadake, in 2009 we continued along the trail directly towards Nakadake Hot Spring, but in 2010 we hiked out to Mt. Araidake (2,183 m = 7,162 ft) and then back to Mt. Mamiyadake and continued on to Nakadake Hot Spring.

The upper photo on the following page shows the very western edge of "Poison Hot Spring Valley" and also shows Mt. Hokuchindake (2,244 m = 7,362 ft) on the left. This photo was taken in 2009 – too bad that we climbed Mt. Hokuchindake in 2010 and were surrounded by clouds. Oh well, such is life. The lower photo on the facing page is zoomed in to Mt. Hokuchindake and in this photo you can actually see the trail which comes down this side of the mountain. Between this point and Mt. Hokuchindake, that other highest point is probably Mt. Nakadake (2,113 m = 6,932 ft). We were atop this peak in both 2009 and 2010, but it was such a minor peak that we did not bother with photos of ourselves at its summit.

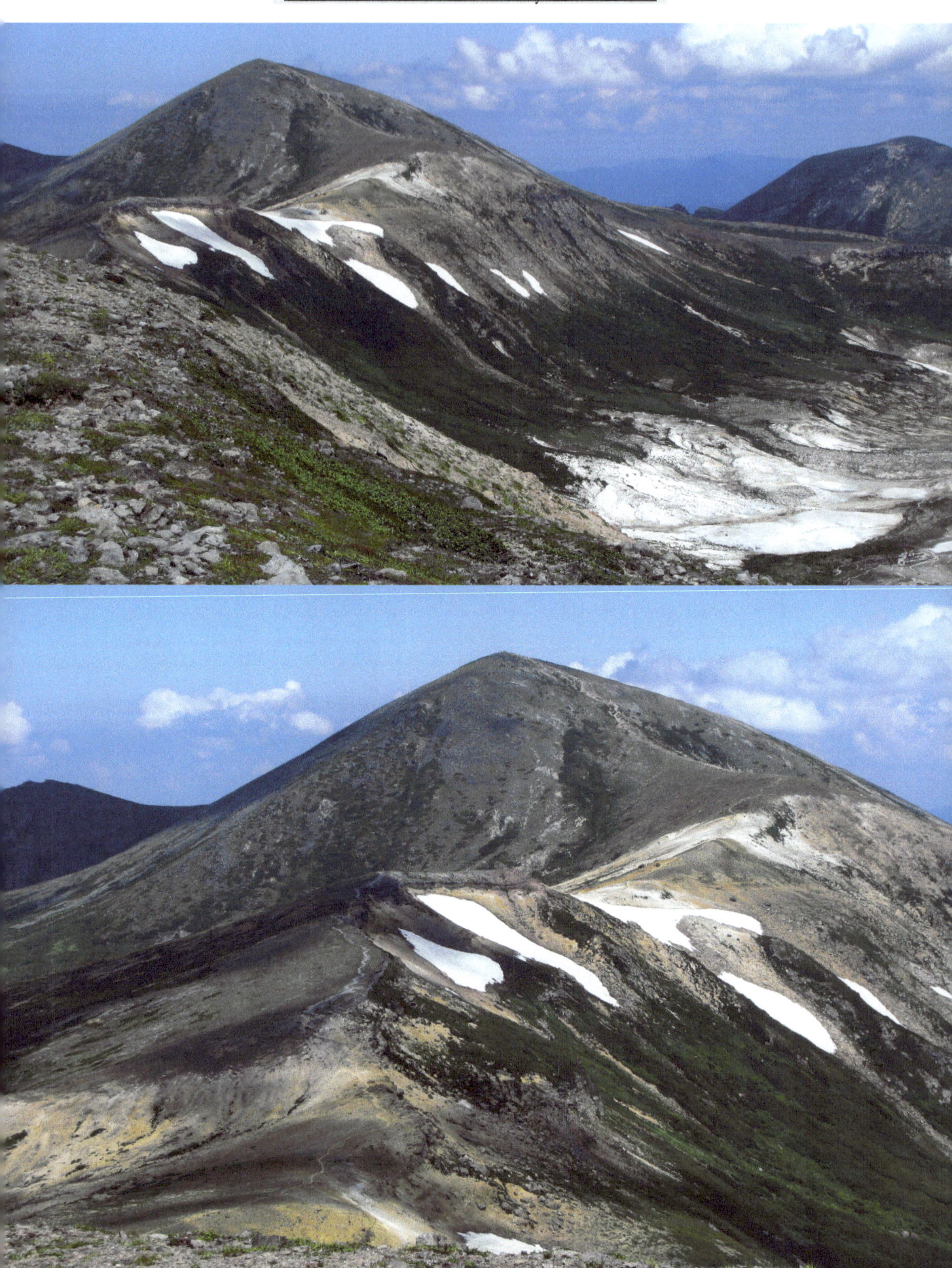

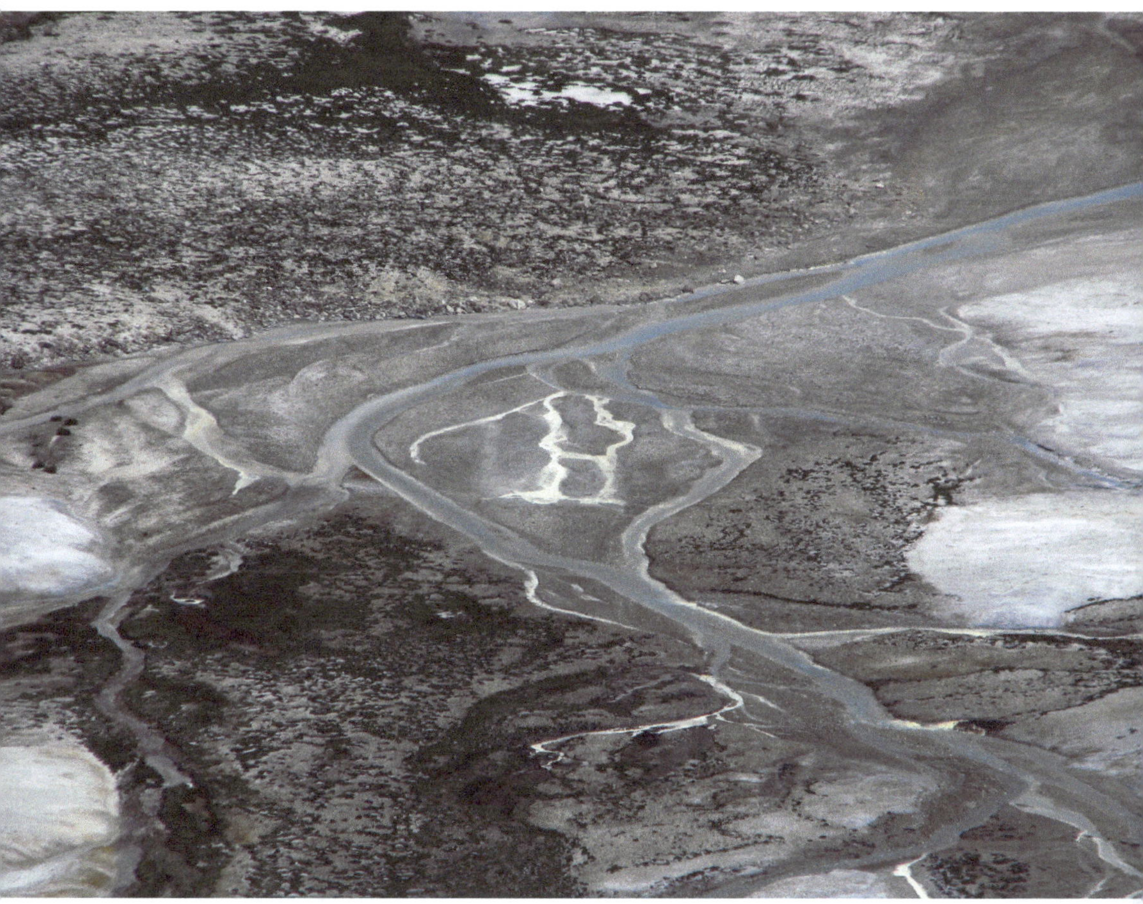

   The photo above gives you a final view down into "Poison Hot Spring Valley". What are those two streams right at about the center of the photo which pop up, seemingly out of nowhere and then flow into the main stream? This does not seem to make sense from a hydrologic standpoint. Near the left side of the photo and about one-third of the way up from the bottom you can see a dark brown area in the center of a green area – what happened here? Is this the result of an extremely hot or poisonous upwelling of hot water which killed the vegetation here? Personally, I have to wonder how much geological exploration, research and detailed mapping has been done here and what was found while they were doing it.

   The upper photo on the following page shows snowdrift scenery along the trail to Nakadake Hot Spring. The lower photo shows the cliff-like walls of the area from which the creek flows. Nakadake Hot Spring is just a short distance below this point and it flows directly into the creek.

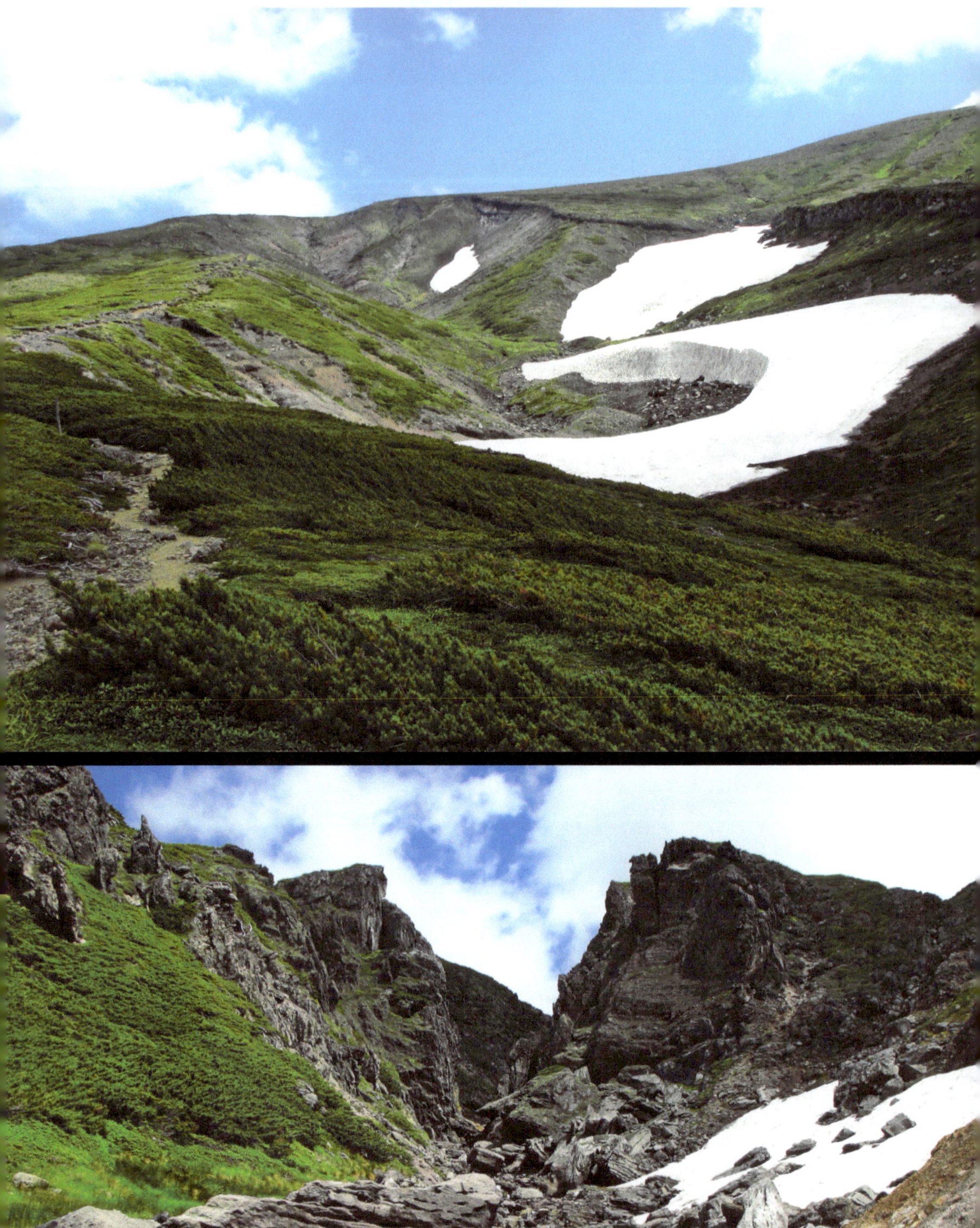

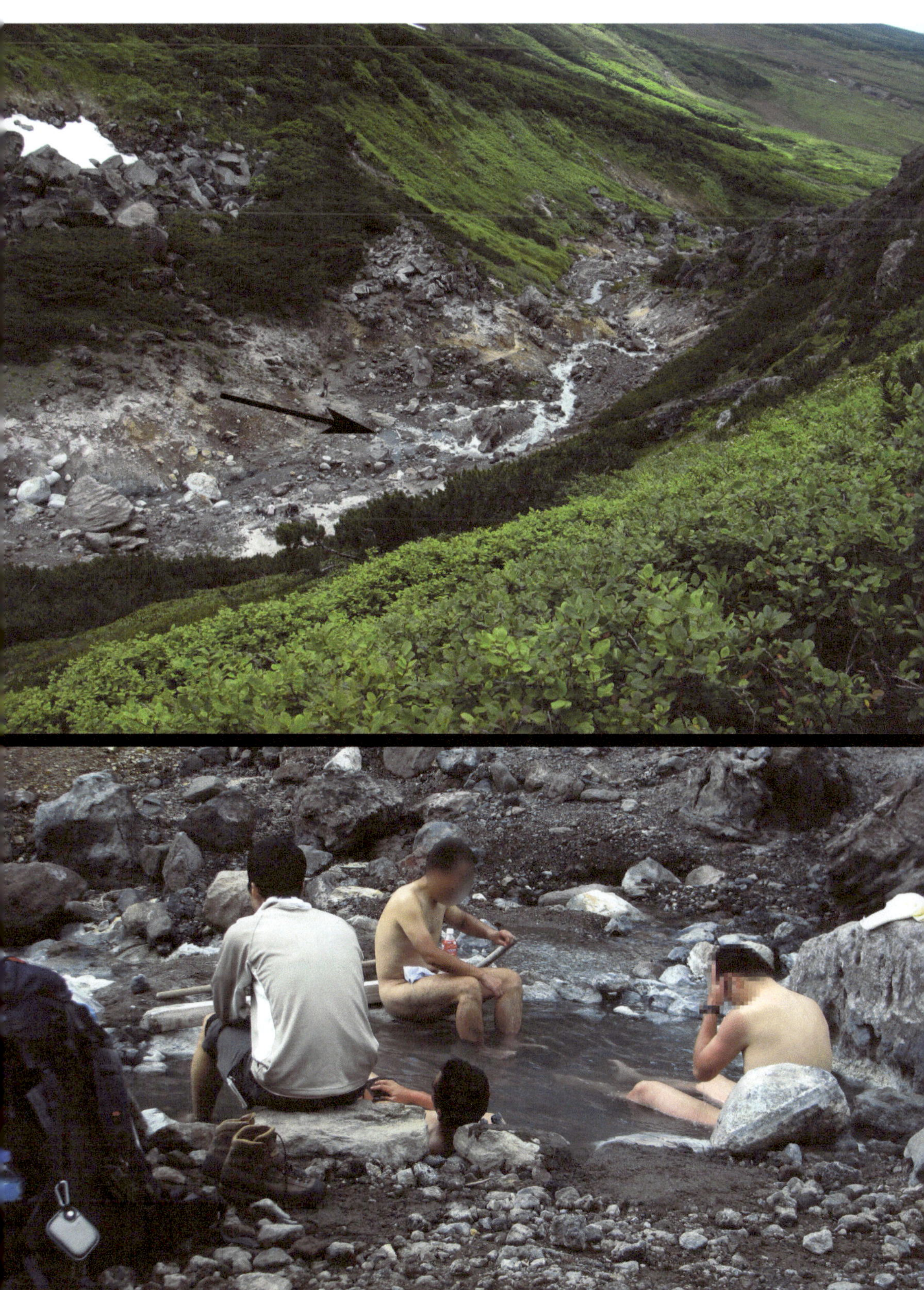

The two photos on the preceding page both show Nakadake On-sen (Hot Spring) (中岳温泉). The upper photo shows the hot spring pool at the end of the black arrow. This photo was actually taken before the lower photo on page 48, but that photo was placed out of sequence because we wanted to show both of these hot spring pool photos on the same page.

The lower photo shows some people taking advantage of the hot spring to clean up a bit and to soak their tired muscles in the hot water. We have passed by this hot spring three times now, once in 2009 and twice in 2010, and we also have taken advantage of it to relax our tired muscles. In the lower photo the faces have been purposely blurred to protect the identity of the naked bathers.

The mountains, if you would call them mountains, in the photo below are very appropriately named Large Mound (right) and Small Mound (left) in English. In Japanese Large Mound is Ootsuka (大塚) and Small Mound is Kozuka (小塚). If you refer back to the map on page 14 once again, these two mounds are located directly above the Nakadake Hot Spring annotation. We are on the trail to the south of the same annotation, so that means we are actually quite far from the mounds. They strike me as very intriguing.

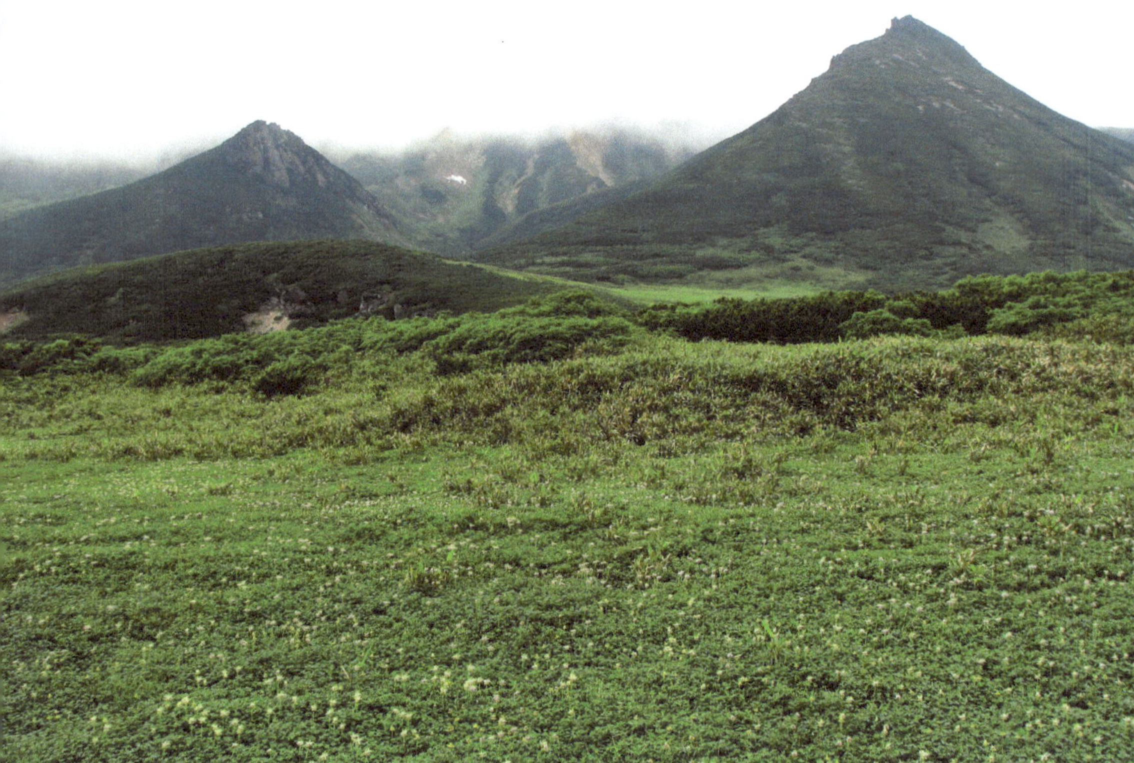

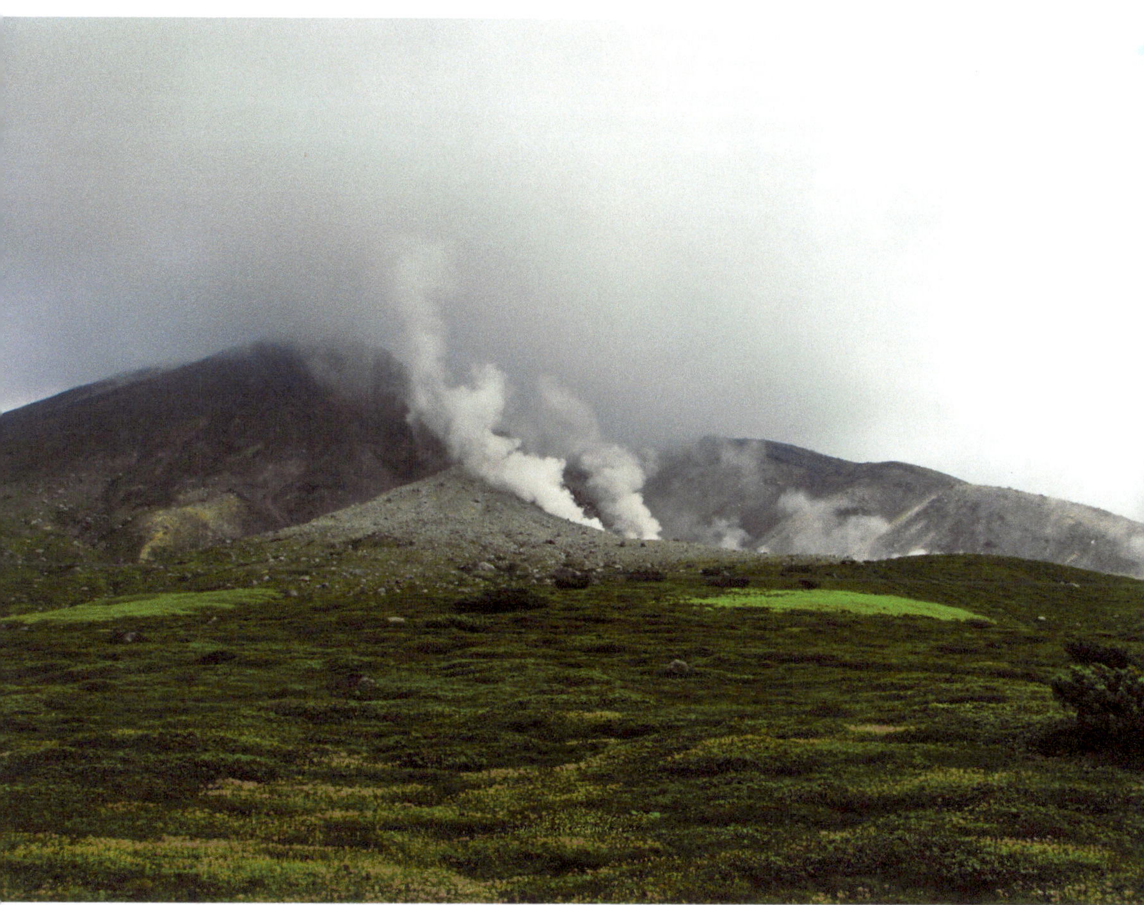

At this point (photo just above) we are hiking along the trail which goes southwest (see left side of map on page 14) just to the right of the annotation which says "Sugatami Pond". We are probably just about at the ✱ mark below the ◀ 1:40 above the "Sugatami Pond" annotation. The ✱ mark indicates a panoramic view spot. We are coming back around and are once again able to see Mt. Asahidake and the smoke rising from the fumaroles. At this point we have just about completed this volume of this series of books; in fact, there is only one photo remaining to show you.

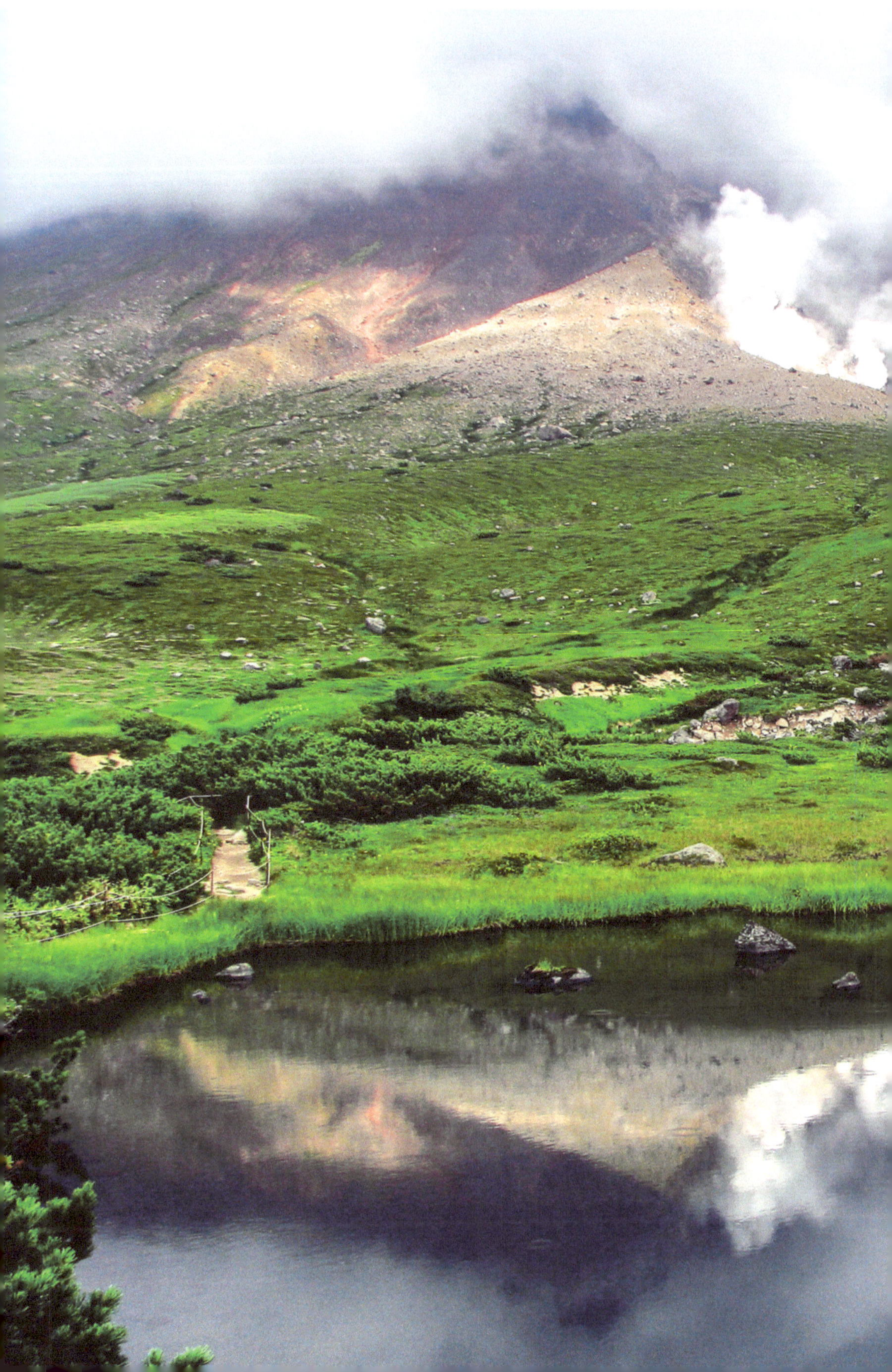

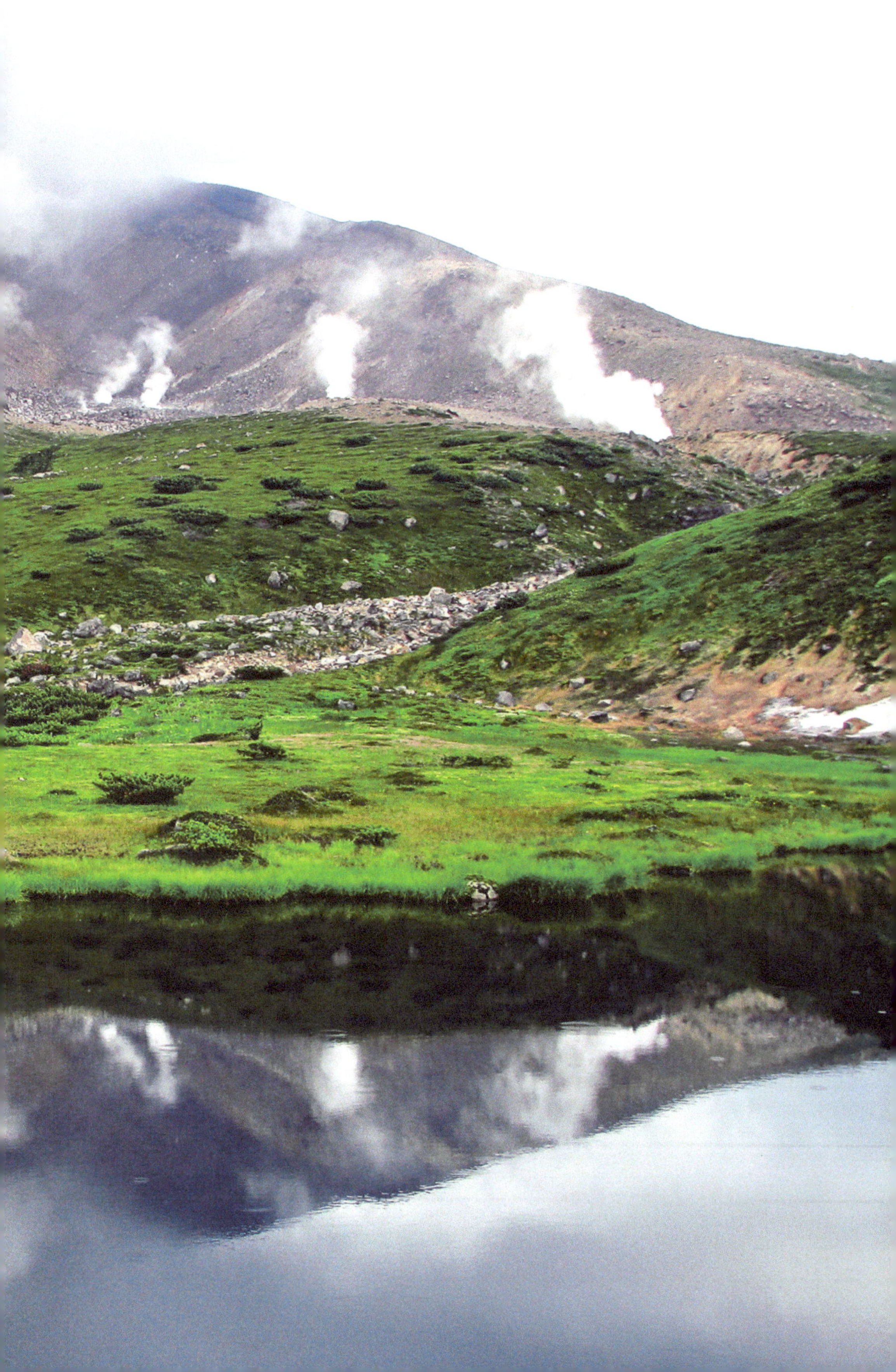

The previous two-page spread is the final photo for Mt. Asahidake. This photo was taken at the point marked "Here" on the small section of map reproduced just below. The reflection of Mt. Asahidake in the pond is magnificent, despite the abundance of clouds.

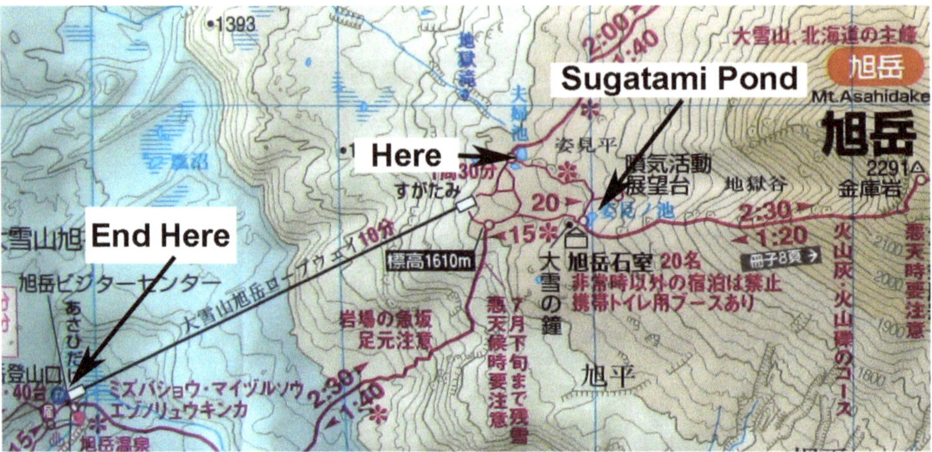

That photo ends Volume 1 of this series of books and we hope that you enjoyed your armchair adventure as much as we enjoyed the actual adventure. The next Volume will take us all to Mt. Chokai (or Choukai) (2,236 m = 7,336 ft) (鳥海山).

We sincerely hope that you are enjoying this series of books. If you would like any further information about any of these mountains there is a great abundance of it available on the internet.

If you want to e-mail me with specific questions you may do so through the link on my website, which is http://danwiz.com. I hope to maintain this site as long as I am alive.

THE END

ABOUT THE AUTHORS

Daniel Wieczorek was born in 1947 in Ionia, Michigan. He graduated from the University of Michigan with a B.S. in Forestry in 1969. He moved to Oregon to work in the field of forestry in 1971. That was followed by a move to Alaska in 1975, where he continued his career in forestry. After about a 14 year career in forestry, Daniel decided to do something different and he served as a Peace Corps Volunteer in The Philippines from 1985 – 1987. Upon completion of his Peace Corps service he returned to Alaska, where he attended the University of Alaska – Fairbanks and received an M.B.A. in 1991. This was followed by a move to South Korea in 1992, where Daniel taught English to Korean people wishing to improve their English Language skills. Daniel's next stop was in New York City, where he worked as temporary staff at Deutsche Bank from 1998 – 2001. He left NYC in March 2001 and moved on to his present home in Mitaka City, Tokyo, Japan. He is teaching English in Japan and at this time he's been teaching as a career for about 17 years. He has been hiking, climbing and doing photography since he was about 12 years old.

Kazuya Numazawa was born in 1979 in Shinjo in Yamagata Prefecture, Japan. He was raised in Funagata Town in Yamagata Prefecture. He graduated from Tokyo University in 2005. Since that time he has worked in several fields, but primarily in Cram Schools around the Mitaka Area.

Daniel and Kazuya met in 2001 and they have been hiking, mountain climbing and doing photography together since that time and generally enjoying life together.

NOTES

PHOTO CREDITS

Daniel's Photos:

Pages 9, 10, 11 bottom, 12, 14, 15 all, 16, 18, 19 top left, 19 bottom, 21 left, 23, 25, 26 all, 27 all, 28, 29, 30, 31, 32 bottom, 33, 34, 35, 37 top, 37 bottom, 38 left, 39 top, 40, 41 all, 42, 44 all, 45 right, 46 all, 47, 48 all, 49 bottom, 50, 51, 52-53, 54.

Kazuya's Photos:

Pages 11 top, 17 all, 19 top right, 20, 21 right, 22, 24 bottom, 32 top, 36, 38 right, 39 bottom, 43, 45 left, 49 top.

Unknown:

Page 24 top.

www.ingramcontent.com/pod-product-compliance
Lightning Source LLC
Chambersburg PA
CBHW041729030726
47636CB00011B/510